W9-BUA-006

THE CONSCIOUS COMMUNICATOR

Making Communication Work In The Work Place

John Brennan
InterAct Communication Concepts

Addison-Wesley Publishing Company
Reading, Massachusetts • Menlo Park, California • London • Don Mills, Ontario

Illustrations by Ned Williams

 Printed in the United States of America. Published simultaneously in Canada. Library of Congress Catalog Card No. 73–14351.

To Peg and Jack:
They know who they are.

Acknowledgments

Some Overdue Dues

A book may begin with its author's idea, an idea which he puts on paper, refines, expands, polishes, and finally submits to critical scrutiny; but it's perhaps more accurate to say that the final product—the book itself—is *made,* rather than written. Between the day of conception and the day of publication a lot of people participate in a process which results in a book. While ultimately the book succeeds or fails on the merits of the author's ideas and his ability to communicate those ideas, he owes some dues to those people who helped provide him the opportunity to either succeed or fail, which is all an author—or anyone else—should ask of another person. It's time now to make a down payment on those dues:

To Ann Detweiler, Joan Passalacqua, and Lenore Steinberg, who patiently and deftly translated and typed my multiple manuscript revisions and thus produced a final draft the editor could comprehend;

To Otto Klima and Ed Curtis of General Electric, for providing me time to collect my thoughts and get them on paper, and for their general support of my efforts;

To Shel Gordon of Stein, Roe & Farnham, and to Maury Davenport of the National Council on Alcoholism—Delaware Valley Area, who once again proved their integrity and friendship, this time by reviewing the manuscript as if it had been written by a stranger;

To William Gallagher of Arthur D. Little, Inc., Robert Jud of Marsh & McLennan, and Donald Sweet of Celanese Corp., none of whom I've met, but to whom I'm grateful for their critical assessment and comments on the manuscript;

To Dick Jackman of General Electric, who wouldn't remember why I owe him dues, but I'll never forget;

And to Dea, whose contribution to the communication climate adds meaning to everything.

Bryn Mawr, Pennsylvania J.B.
January 1974

Contents

PART TWO
ORGANIZATION CLIMATE:
MYSTERIES, MYTHS, AND MODELS

7 / Mysteries

8 / Myths

Part One

ANYONE CAN COMMUNICATE BECAUSE EVERYONE IS A COMMUNICATOR

Prologue:
The View From The Bridge

We live in Corporate America. Most of us work for organizations. None of us escapes their influence. No, this isn't a social tract on the American way of life, not in the usual sense. But it is about organizational life, and it does address social matters in that context. Organizations are, after all, small societies, and working surely is a social experience.

Communication is the glue that holds a society together. The ability to communicate enables people to form and maintain personal relationships. And the quality of such relationships depends on the caliber of communication between the parties.

Personal relationship is what organizations are all about—or should be. An organization, whatever its size, mission, or motive, is merely a collection of people assembled to pursue a common objective. An organization functions through its people, who in turn function through communication. What could be simpler? Almost anything.

We live at a time when information gushing from the mass media involves us in the affairs of our society—indeed, in those of the world society—with or without our consent. Paradoxically, the smaller societies—our organizations—are routinely accused of clinging to communication practices that clash with employe expectations energized outside the work place. Too often the charges are true. With grim regularity, the inability or unwillingness of managers to adjust to social reality stifles the very relationships that are vital to a healthy enterprise.

"Profitable" and "healthy" are not synonyms. If it were otherwise, not so many of the companies reporting record profits would also be hot with the fever of employe discontent. But there are many such firms, and regardless of their current financial condition, they are sick corporate bodies.

The argument here is not against profits; rather it's for an enlightened management effort to make the work environment more pleasant and the work experience more satisfying. Most employes and managers alike would probably welcome the improvement. And such an effort is entirely compatible with the profit motive. Indeed, if people got more out of their jobs, it's likely that they'd put more into them.

But employes won't put more into their jobs until they're given the opportunity to do so. And they won't get the opportunity until managers grasp the obvious social reality that so far has eluded so many of us. It's the work experience, not the work ethic, that's in trouble. People don't necessarily hate work. In fact, most seem to realize that they need it for psychological and social as well as economic reasons. They don't dislike having something to do, they abhor having nothing to say about how things get done. The issue is involvement, not control. The goal is participation, not anarchy.

As citizens and consumers, people are accorded the flattery attendant to the hustle of a vote or a buck. As employes, however, these same people usually have no vote, not even in matters affecting their own jobs. Their opinions and concerns are often met by indifference—or worse, chilling condescension. And their approval, so cherished in the market place, is seldom sought in the work place—except, of course, in times of organizational crisis.

Predictably, such conflicts nurture adversary, rather than cooperative, relationships between employes and their employers. It's bad enough to revoke a person's sense of citizenship, but when you deny his adulthood as well, you're bound to create resentment. Perhaps it's this resentment that underlies the charges that organizations are dehumanizing and impersonalizing. No doubt, *dehumanizing* aptly suits the management style of some organizations, and *impersonalizing* fits many. However, for purposes of generalization, the term that best characterizes most organizations—if not the vast majority—is *infantilizing*: They are places in which adults are treated like children. Not only is participation unduly restricted, even information—which people require to perform their jobs properly, to engender positive feelings between themselves and their employers, and to achieve some measure of psychic satisfaction—is rationed as if too much candy would make the kids sick. A lot of the kids are getting sick anyhow, but it's from malnutrition.

Even children occasionally resent being treated like children. But they get over it. Most adults, and all healthy ones, who are continually infantilized don't get over it. They become hostile. Some complain, some become disruptive. Many drop out. Where do they go? Most are on someone's payroll. It's just that they do little or no work. Indeed, most of the unemployed people in America are on someone's payroll.

As managers, it's easy for us to blame employes, or any other handy source, for the many malfunctions that plague our organizational life. It's easy because we've had so much practice at it. All we need do is continue to arbitrarily assign malevolent motives and child-like characteristics to those veritable strangers we call employes. That way, we can avoid the difficult and time-consuming effort involved in getting to know them as individuals. Thus we can have the necessary personal contact with employes, but still not be bothered by interpersonal relationships with them.

Alternatively, we can adjust our own policies and practices. We can personalize communication in the work place. This approach is tougher, but more useful and infinitely more rewarding.

Communication is personalized when management practices reflect an understanding that the employe group is composed of *individual* people, each with a distinct personality.

Communication is personalized when managers take the time and exert the effort to show some concern for the individual interests, needs, motives and aspirations of their employes.

Communication is personalized when managers and employes identify with each other—and thus with the organization.

But to accomplish this, people must know each other and care about each other. In short, relationships in the work place should resemble those we seek in our personal life. And why not? All of life is personal, including work. One-third of most days and about two-thirds of most lifetimes are devoted to working.

What's often called the "man/manager interface" marks the place where positive, personalized relationships between employes and their employers are either established or stifled. Where such associations manifest mutual respect, they usually are healthy and productive. Where the parties recognize that their roles carry different responsibilities and rewards, but that each role and each person has worth, the relationship is rewarding in itself. Where managers accept the reality that employe goals and aspirations are as important to them as individuals as corporate objectives are to the entity, the relationship can be an asset to the institution. Such relationships diminish work-related anxiety and make the work day pass fairly pleasantly.

Most of the blame and little of the credit for an organization's operations falls on what's generally labeled "middle management." All middle managers have at least one thing in common: they are truly the managers in the middle.

Middle managers are responsible to top management for an organization's day-to-day operations. Concurrently, they're accountable—in a very real and often trying way—to employes as well. Clearly, employes identify with their organization, in either a positive or negative sense, through their immediate boss. And the vast majority of employes work for a middle-manager whose behavior presumably reflects the attitudes of the entire organization toward relationships with employes.

Who, then, is a supervisor? Here's an even stickier semantic problem.

A supervisor is actually anyone who supervises the work of other employes. However, the term has acquired a more restrictive meaning. Generally, it's used to designate one who serves as a straw boss or work leader. In many places, if not most, it denotes the first rung on the management ladder. Presumably, supervisors and foremen have about the same organizational standing.

Rather than placidly accepting the unacceptable, let's say simply that for our purposes, supervisors belong to middle management and their role is to supervise people. There's a reason for the distinction.

At some point, a manager's ascension of the corporate ladder takes him out of daily contact with employes. Comparatively, then, senior executives tend to manage paper, while supervisors manage people. But supervisors can't go it alone. In corporate America people need organizations; but more importantly, organizations need productive people with healthy attitudes. Mythology notwithstanding, managers do not have all the good ideas, nor the only healthy attitudes about what constitutes either organizational or employe prosperity.

Top managers who are tuned in to this reality carefully select their supervisors. And they willingly support their supervisors' efforts to build mutually rewarding relationships with employes. They do this through encouragement, through training, and by providing supervisors with sufficient information to respond honestly and intelligently to employe concerns. The combination of senior management's interest, assistance, and sharing of information helps supervisors develop positive, personalized relationships with employes. These, in turn, create a work environment in which people can identify with the organization and its goals without abandoning their personal identity or individual goals.

Such an environment breeds understanding and reduces exploitation on both sides: management's and the employes', and the result is a climate conducive to communication. Such a setting also obviates the need for "crisis communications."

Characteristically, in periods of threat—an economic downturn, a competitor's charge, a union's drive for recognition and membership—organizations resort to "crisis communications" programs. They expend tremendous quantities of energy and other resources trying to convince employes that everything will be all right if only they work harder, remain loyal to the organization, and have faith that their devotion will be rewarded. This, of course, should be going on all the time, not merely in times of turmoil.

Employes will usually reject the notion that they're part of a big, happy team, all whistling and working together to slay some menacing dragon, unless they've been made to feel like management's teammates all along. If they haven't been, they'll usually respond with either hostility or apathy. To the wary and the wise, both are media of communication.

Supervisors form both the first and last line of defense against employe apathy and discontent. Where relationships at this interface are rewarding to individuals, organizational health —however measured—is enhanced.

This book, then, is for supervisors.

It's also for anyone else who might be intrigued by the possibilities for better professional relationships, which frequently result in the achievement of more work with less hassle.

Sound manipulative? Judge for yourself. But put work relationships into the same context as other social experiences and contacts. We're all givers, we're all takers. And we like balanced relationships best.

Through communication we develop relationships, through relationships we acquire understanding of one another, through such understanding we improve our organizations. In this book, communication, relationships, understanding, and a healthy organizational climate are virtually synonymous.

Supervisors and others charged with creating a climate in which communication flourishes are presumably busy people. Therefore, the book is designed for rapid reading. It's conversational and fairly informal.

Now here's what the book is not: It isn't a textbook in the usual sense. It's not intended to tell you everything you need to know about communication. Rather, it aims to remind you of much you already know but, if you're reasonably normal, probably ignore or disregard.

Unlike a textbook, one chapter does not always directly relate or lead to the next. More like articles, each chapter represents a unit of thought; each one, regardless of length, says what needs to be said. Obviously, a highly subjective judgment.

Just as the chapters should be considered units, the two parts are units. Read them, digest them, and the strategy will be clear. Whether or not you agree with it, at least be assured that in deference to your time and other demands I've tried to facilitate your reading and recall.

Many readers will encounter what for them is new information. Hopefully, all will achieve a new or improved perspective. There aren't any short-cuts: First we have to think, then we can learn to communicate better with others.

Part I is mostly about thinking, or perhaps more accurately, reflecting on what communication is and is not—how we achieve it, how we so often preclude it.

Part II continues this theme in the chapters on Mysteries and Myths. These essentially deal with some insidious ways in which we manage to rip-off ourselves and others in the name of efficiency, security, and organizational order.

For "how to" book fans, Part II also offers a number of models for evaluating one's own and the organization's behavior, plotting career progress, and improving the communication climate.

Certain readers may sense a bit of Utopianism here. So be it. But the view from the bridge reveals many organizations struggling against the choppy waters of discontent, navigating with a faulty compass which communication could repair. Others, however, needn't follow this course. The Conscious Communicator offers a practical alternative to heeding the voices of despair which today shout to society and its institutions: Jump!

Chapter 1

In The Beginning Was The Word. . . But No Communication

Right at the outset we were in trouble.

The Garden of Eden may seem an unlikely setting for history's first man/manager communication breakdown, but perhaps even paradise wasn't perfect. Unfortunately, our Eden bureau chief was away at the time on another assignment, but later, in an exclusive interview from "somewhere in exile," he got the following account from Eve.

"The instructions Adam got were pretty fuzzy, if you ask me," Eve said. "But as best I can put the story together The Boss said something like 'Don't touch the forbidden fruit,' or 'Don't take any apples.' As it turned out, what he meant was 'Don't fool around with Eve.' Who knew?" she added with a shrug.

"Well, you can imagine poor Adam—confused and all by that kind of communication," Eve continued. "It isn't right. You shouldn't have to guess at what The Boss means. But that's typical of this place. You don't understand what's going on half the time," she said.

Eve characterized the subsequent disciplinary decision as "a classic case of Management overreaction. Boy, was He bugged," she remarked.

Summing up the situation, Eve said it was clear that "Adam got The Word but missed The Message." Although she sympathized with Adam's dilemma, noting that he was new on the job, Eve decried her own exclusion from the decision-making process. She said that until now no one had shown any interest in her version of the events. "Nobody ever asks *me* anything," she lamented. "Tell, tell, tell, all the time tell! Nobody says, 'How do you feel, Eve?' Or, 'What's your story, Eve?' What kind of outfit is this, anyway?"

On learning that she would be quoted directly rather than having her comments attributed to "a highly reliable source," Eve expressed some concern, saying, "Here we go again. Now I'll probably be labeled 'just another long-haired malcontent,' but what the heck—I'm tired of being ripped-off by The System."

Eve thanked the reporter for his time and concern. Then, demurely adjusting her fig leaf, she sauntered off. You guessed it. She headed directly toward a nearby grove of apple trees.

Chapter 2

Retreat From Reality

Whodunnit?

The Communication Problem syndrome is the biggest copout since the serpent split, leaving Adam and Eve holding the bag—or the core, as the case may be.

How often do you hear it said when something goes wrong, "There was simply a communication problem"? How often do *you* fire off and fall back on such platitudes? There are other versions of course. Some perennial favorites include: "I guess communication just broke down," and, "If only communication was better around here, this wouldn't have happened."

Such statements have at least two things in common: they provide no information whatsoever about why something went wrong; they offer no hope that similar difficulties will be avoided in the future. Furthermore, as in the case of Eve and Eden's management, where people fail to identify with the problem, it's unlikely that they'll feel responsible for the solution.

There's often an attitude of resignation accompanying reports of communication problems. And not infrequently the dialogue is augmented by suitable stage gestures—a kind of Alfred E.

Neuman (MAD Magazine) smile, or a shrugging of shoulders—suggesting that despite a letter-perfect performance by everyone involved (particularly the speaker), some cosmic force intervened, visiting delay, disorder, or even defeat on the project under discussion. For background music, perhaps the staccato strains of "Blame It On The Bossa Nova" might be most appropriate. Certainly we can't blame communication problems on *people.* And assuredly we can't blame them on ourselves. Or can we?

Whether or not you can depends on you, your hang-ups, your degree of insightfulness. True, communication breaks down when somebody fails to get your message, but this often occurs because—despite appearances and good intentions—you haven't *sent* any message. At least nothing that's discernable as a message. Put another way, when a communication problem arises, it isn't always the other guy (the one we tend to think of as the receiver) who's at fault.

Obviously, you can't fix a problem if you deny its existence. Nor can you deal properly with the resulting failure unless you examine and evaluate your role in it. It's never pleasant to acknowledge responsibility for a failure even to yourself, let alone to others, but it is necessary. To relentlessly pretend that Providence, others, or the Bossa Nova are always to blame assures reinforcement of the failure, not its repair.

A Catholic priest tells the story of an elderly parishioner who complained to him about her husband. She concluded her litany of the husband's sins by saying, "Father, you really must get him to come to confession." "Why?" countered the puzzled and somewhat irritated priest. "You've already confessed quite enough for the poor man."

Other versions of this scene are enacted every day in our offices, shops, conferences, and social seminars (cocktail parties). When the topic turns to organizations, the places where most of us work, a discussion of communication practices and problems frequently ensues. Typically, however, the conversation travels over, under, around, and through the subject without ever settling atop the real problems. Seldom is anything of lasting value accomplished.

Such conversations may be therapeutic, but they're all form with little positive function. Everyone reinforces everyone else's self-concept through a kind of noncompetitive "can you top this?" Unquestionably, there are communication problems in our organizations. Almost everyone will admit to them, regardless of his organizational position. Many will readily confess all manner of sins and identify the sinners: their boss, employes, or associates; the customers, stockholders, or government. But never oneself. You keep waiting for the other shoe to drop, but it seldom does. Perhaps contentment *is* an elderly parishioner. The priest never did say if she found time for a *mea culpa* or two on her own behalf.

One Against Many

Run your own experiment. The next time you're in a conversation with some friends or associates who work in organizations, including your own, ask if they're aware of any communication problems. See if you don't get a resounding "You'd better believe it" for a reply. See also if the conversational undercurrent doesn't flow toward something like "Here's all the stuff I'm doing to make the place run better but because of those noncommunicative dummies who surround me I'm hopelessly overworked and getting more frustrated every day."

Next, ask three questions: "What is your definition of communication? What is your approach to communicating with other people? What is your technique for getting better cooperation from all those noncommunicative dummies?" Then watch the shoulders shrug. "What can I do? I'm only one person."

Suddenly, it's out in the open. It's *me* against them, and their superior numbers result in an inertial problem which I, despite the righteousness of my cause and the correctness of my course, can't even hope to overcome! Only grudgingly might it be conceded that each of *them* could be thinking precisely the same thing about *me*. But that's silly. Such a contention obviously would be preposterous. Or would it?

The Inevitability Copout

There seems also to be a sort of "notion of inevitability" associated with so-called communication problems. And this is among the chief impediments to communication between and among people. The notion—or more accurately, the practices it engenders—provides us with a built-in predisposition to accept

communication failures as we do the occasional inconvenience of snow and rain. No one's fault. Just happens. On the other hand, when blame must be assigned, and for some reason the Bossa Nova won't do, there's always The Organization and all those other people standing by. Handy, huh?

The notion of inevitability includes the "to err is human" rationalization. This is almost like resorting to the truth. But not quite. We use it when trapped.

The cop's got you pulled over to the side of the highway. You were speeding. You were not on an emergency run to the hospital, being tailgated by another vehicle, or forced to speed up in order to avoid an accident. You've been through your entire repertoire of fantasy and fiction, but the cop is not impressed.

His ticket book and T-Ball Jotter remain at the ready. What now? The old give-a-guy-a-break-'cause-after-all-we're-only-human-and-we-all-make-mistakes play.

Not very creative, but accurate, and occasionally effective. Sometimes this gambit works; usually it doesn't, at least not with policemen. Bosses and associates are another audience and often another story. Maybe it has something to do with familiarity and future expectations.

The cop presumably doesn't know you. He has little reason to expect that he'll see you again, except perhaps under similar circumstances. However, in that event he'll again be in command of the situation. In contrast, your boss and associates work with you every day. They know you. More importantly, they know that you know them.

Consider now a different kind of violation—a breakdown in communication for which you are responsible. Compare your position with the policeman to your position with your boss and associates. While the former is secure in his, the latter are not in theirs.

Each in their own way, and at some level of consciousness, your boss and associates know that one day they'll be in a similar bind; will somehow be implicated in a failure; will in some way require your help or support. So while the cop gives you a ticket, which you'll pay for, the others are acquiring "tickets" which they have some expectation of "cashing in" at a future date. This may seem nice and normal, even humane. However, what all too frequently happens is that the tickets are exchanged but no lessons are learned from the experience.

Yes, there was a communication problem. Yes, this did result in a deviation from the plan or a disruption of certain work processes. Yes, you are the party responsible. "But, gee whiz, boss; golly, guys—these things happen, right? I mean, what with *everybody* so busy, and all." (The use of *everybody* provides a cozy shelter. Under such circumstances there's safety and security in *everybody*; only loneliness in *I* and *me*.)

The confession becomes its own absolution. The sin is no longer what it seemed to have been. No longer are we dealing with a transgression which either stemmed from or resulted in improper job performance; instead we have a confession of humanness, a declaration which merely admits human frailty. Obviously, no sin at all.

That which is everyone's failing is no one's fault.

However, finding fault, identifying the specific reasons for problems in communication and in other functions which falter when communication fails to occur is an essential task for everyone associated with or affected by such problems. At one time or another, this imposes an obligation on everyone in an organization. While people must be treated humanely, problems must be dealt with brutally. And the obvious place for each of us to begin is with ourselves.

The objective should never be blame for blame's sake. Don't accept it if it's not yours, don't dispense it if it is. But know the difference. The idea is to fix the problem, then go on to the next one which is probably there awaiting your attention.

We must reject the notion of inevitability—a misconception which too often permeates our thinking and, consequently, perpetuates our failure as communicators. Unless and until we do this, events, rather than our own actions, will continue to dominate our lives.

The Unsweetened Truth

"Everything went flawlessly, except we had a breakdown in communication." No matter how you try to sweeten it with euphemisms, the translation for that is: "We failed." Things did not go according to plan. Sometimes the failure is crucial, sometimes it's only mildly aggravating. But usually it's avoidable.

Imagine yourself as a sales manager who gets this message one day: "The big deal's closed, boss. Negotiations went perfectly. Well, almost perfectly. One small hitch. We forgot to get the customer to sign the contract—before he died." Admittedly, this is not your run-of-the-mill occurrence. But how many deals die, or are never born, because someone fails to follow through on an assignment?

Surely someone had, or was supposed to have had, responsibility for putting the pen in the customer's hand. Now, if you're the sales manager, what's your line? What do you say to the employe? To your boss? More importantly, what action do you take to lessen the likelihood of recurrence?

What you don't do is nothing. And certainly, if you're smart, you don't shrug off the affair with a torrent of clichés. Presumably you start looking for what went wrong—hopefully, beginning with a mirror.

The extreme alternative is to cop out, quickly and completely; to deny responsibility, publicly and privately. Blame everyone else involved. This frequently practiced procedure is not only self-defeating, it's easily overwhelmed by just one question from your boss: Who is the supervisor who presided over the failure?

Rationalization and denial are a pair of rubber crutches. In time, neither the person who leans on them nor the person who lets him will be able to stand up straight.

There are reasons why things sometimes go wrong. These can be uncovered and understood. Corrective actions can and must be taken by all of us if our personal and working lives are to become more rewarding.

Consistent inattention to communication, its functions and malfunctions, hampers the efficiency and profitability of our organizations and stifles the development of those who inhabit them. As long as we ignore, rationalize, or deny our failures as communicators, for that long will we shrink from responsibility rather than grow toward our intellectual, emotional, and contributive potential.

Chapter 3

The Truth About Harry

Look Beneath the Surface

Communication problems don't wear labels. Worse yet, they generally are masked by failures in other functions. You'll find this effect in a variety of individual and institutional activities.

Some illustrations:

- Two people have a disagreement which leads to the termination of their relationship.
- A driver ignores a red light and collides with another vehicle.
- A quarterback throws a post-pattern pass as the flanker runs a down-and-out pattern, resulting in an incompletion or even an interception.
- An electronics manufacturer produces computers at one location and peripheral equipment at another; but when the components are brought together to make a system they are found to be incompatible.
- And remember the unsigned contract from Chapter Two?

In each case, you can readily identify a failure in some function other than communication. In each case there would seem to have been an intention, a plan, or a design for something to occur other than in the way it did.

In each case, someone (or a lot of someones) wasn't given, missed, or ignored a signal; failed to get, understand, or act on a message.

On the surface, you can observe the effect of the failures: the antagonists who now avoid one another even when circumstances place them in the same room; the wrecked vehicles; the "busted play"; the lifeless equipment surrounding the computer; the vacant space where a signature should be. What you usually don't see is the failure in communication. You'll have to dig for that, but it's there.

Faulty communication lurks behind every failure in function. Occasionally, we get lucky and merely have to scratch the surface to unearth the communication problem. For example: Your boss asks you for a report. He wants it by Monday afternoon. You tell Harry, one of your employes, to prepare the report and give it to you by Monday morning. That should permit plenty of time for your review and any necessary adjustments. Plenty of time.

"You understand, Harry? Monday morning." Harry nods his head up and down. "Right," says Harry, "Monday morning."

Monday morning arrives—but the report doesn't. Monday afternoon your boss calls you for the report. You call Harry, who announces, "I thought you said Tuesday."

Don't bother to tell your boss about Harry. He'll only think you're an idiot too.

What do you do for an encore? Harry's is a tough act to follow. So before proceeding, think about it.

The world—and your organization—is filled with Harrys. In fact, there's a little bit of Harry in each of us. He, and we, perform as a result of what we've learned: what will work, what won't. This is part of our survival training, some of which we

acquire by observing our supervisor's behavior. At this point, that may be an unpleasant perspective, but it is a necessary one.

Harry's not the village freak. He's one of us. And his behavior is quite normal by contemporary standards.

When confronted with the preceding situation your choices appear limited. You know what Harry said isn't true. You may even believe he's lying. But how can you say he's lying about what he *thought?* Collaterally, how can you accept the notion that Harry's really as stupid as he now appears to be? This is especially vexing if *you* hired the guy. His seeming stupidity is a reflection on your judgment.

Consider this angle: Harry knows he's lying. You know he's lying. And each of you knows that the other knows. But who can prove anything? And what would you do about it if you could? It was only a simple report.

The Cosmetic Approach

Most of us would probably deal with the surface effect and ignore the real problem. Call this the cosmetic approach. For instance, Harry may have been behind on another assignment, due soon. He genuinely may have believed that despite the pressure of the other assignment he could and would have your report ready on time. Now, having failed to do so, he feels threatened.

Much more serious than the failure in the surface function (no report), is the failure in communication, and thus in the relationship between you and Harry. It's easy to gaze at your empty hand and see calluses instead of the report. What's not so easy to perceive is the possibility that Harry doesn't trust you enough to tell you the truth or to ask for your help. Rather, he falls back on the old "to err is human" rationalization, which in this case comes out sounding something like, "I'm sure you're right, boss; but somehow I got confused and *thought the wrong thing*."

The cosmetic approach may go approximately this way in the various situations mentioned earlier.

- The two who have disagreed avoid each other, ignore the problem. The relationship goes away, but if it was previously a good one then both parties have lost something of value.
- The careless driver gets a ticket; perhaps his auto insurance is cancelled.
- The quarterback "chews out" the flanker, who may remain convinced that he ran the correct pattern, and may now believe that the quarterback is making him a scapegoat.
- Speaking of scapegoats, the electronics manufacturer's top management fires, transfers, or otherwise shakes up some low-level or middle-management people, then congratulates itself for having fixed another major problem.

- The sales manager behaves similarly to the quarterback, while his salesmen duplicate the flanker's attitude and Harry's performance.
- And what about you and Harry? Well, Harry's Harry—can't do much about that, you figure. Conceivably, you'll dump some fantasy on your boss, thus buying more time to either do the report yourself or have another of your employes take a shot at it. The situation with Harry loses importance once the crunch with the boss passes. Harry fades from the immediate picture; neither he nor his performance has priority at this point. A momentary crisis is dismissed as a trivial incident, obviating any expenditure of time or effort to learn the truth about Harry or about yourself. Case closed—until the next time, the next gimmick, the next manifestation of communication failure.

Cosmetic treatment of failures in communication creates the illusion of constructive activity and accomplishment. Consequently, such actions often are regarded as solutions. However, their net effect is to conceal the dynamics which occasion the failures.

Simplistic answers don't solve complex problems, and while cosmetic treatment generally is simplistic, all communication problems are complex. Treating the effect while ignoring the ailment generates more ailments rather than cures.

"Complex" Needn't Mean "Confusing"

Communication is always complex because human beings are complex creatures. Our relationships, whether they involve one person or a multitude, are complex transactions. Our motives, attitudes, and the real reasons for our reactions to messages from others almost never lie on the surface. Only rarely do we take other people, their words and actions, at face value. And seldom do we pause to reevaluate our own motives, attitudes, and behavior. Nor do we devote much time to examining the

dynamics of resistance and rejection as they affect our efforts to communicate with others.

While in certain circumstances communication may appear straightforward, the process through which it occurs—if it occurs—is not. For instance, a directive from a superior to a subordinate seems simple enough. "Do that!" (whatever *that* may be) is a direct and presumably uncomplicated statement. However, it's only a verbalization, a result of the superior's having run certain material through his own thought process to arrive at the conclusion that a particular action must be taken. He issues his order, but still there's no communication. The subordinate has yet to react or respond. At this stage we not only don't know *how* he'll respond, we don't know *if* he'll respond. We're not even sure he got the message. A seemingly simple matter is suddenly an obviously complex situation —made more so if the subordinate replicates Harry's performance. "Oh, you said *that*? I thought you meant *this*."

The situation is further complicated by our routine failure to grasp the essence of the communication process, and by our unwitting insistence on confusing the action (giving an order, relaying information, asking a question) with the intended result: communication.

While the communication process is complex, it needn't be confusing. We just make it that way by failing to deal consciously with human factors which are common to all of us. The communication process begins, ends, succeeds, fails with *people*—not in masses, as individuals.

Relationships

People may change their clothes at the plant, but not their personalities. Their thoughts, feelings, ambitions, fears, and needs are not deposited at the door. Being parts of personality, those things travel with each person. And each person's experiences during a day in his working life go home with him.

It seems incontrovertible that major relationships—those affecting a person's self-concept—intervene in all other relationships.

A person whose self-concept is enhanced by his major relationships (and work is surely one of them) will be less dismayed, sometimes relatively unperturbed, by problems and failures in less vital relationships. Conversely, a person whose self-concept is damaged, or whose emotional safety and security are threatened, will have difficulty in forming or maintaining any positive relationship.

The word *organization* implies interpersonal relationships. The same is true for its companion terms *employe* and *supervisor*.

The basis for interpersonal relationships resides in the very concept of organization. Remove the requirement that people band together to accomplish some common objective and there's no purpose for having an organization.

On the day an organization opens for business, relationships are there waiting to be formed. What's uncertain, however, is what kind of relationships they will be. Will those among employes themselves and between employes and management be rich ones or poor ones? Will they be conducive to the attainment of corporate objectives? Or will they impede, even preclude, their accomplishment? Will people work *with* each other and with their management? Or will they work despite them in order to secure some solely personal rewards? In each instance, the answer rests on how well we understand communication and how wisely we use it.

Borrow Some Shoes

Communication with another person requires that we occasionally walk a mile in his shoes. Even one block would be helpful. Unfortunately, we tend to ignore this crucial requirement, since it impinges on our own ego drives and demands an expenditure of energy and effort we're only infrequently willing to commit.

The general condition of communication indicates that not only don't many of us do much walking, we seldom try on the shoes for size. Ironically, we're quick to criticize the state of communication but reluctant to assume any responsibility for it. We readily identify the flaws in others, but fail to see that our own selfishness and laziness prevents us from utilizing the tools which our ability to communicate places at our disposal.

Admittedly, it's always easier to find the faults in others than in ourselves. However, the achievement of communication within our respective organizations demands that we occasionally look inside ourselves just to be certain that our behavior corresponds with our stated objectives.

Our own ideas and emotions, and the words we use to express them, usually seem of paramount importance to us. As they occupy top—and sometimes sole—priority for us, we often erroneously expect that they should hold a similar rank with others. Consequently, we may regard the ideas, emotions, and words of others as something of an interference. How can communication occur in such circumstances? It can't.

How often do we go about our daily business with a sort of ego chip on our shoulder, in a sense defying others to knock if off? "Just try to change my mind, make me see your views, understand how you feel! Just try to get me to do what you want!"

If we relied on our ears as often as we do our mouths; if our sensing devices were as active as our projective devices, we'd have far fewer difficulties in getting along with one another. We'd also have less reason to complain about communication while rationalizing our own failures.

Communication pervades all human behavior and every interpersonal activity. Consequently, there's no realistic way to segregate communication from getting along with one another. Would you try to separate life from living, actions from behavior, people from personality?

As individuals, and as organization managers, we've got to make some decisions regarding our relationships. Shall we ignore our knowledge of people and their communication requirements and thus complicate, confuse, and sometimes corrupt the quality of our existence? Or shall we employ what we know to improve understanding and enhance relationships in the work place?

We can have it either way, but not both ways simultaneously.

Chapter 4

Speaking of Systems

Information Processing

Man is a communication system. This system acquires and dispenses information. In our society, which runs on information, these are often complex activities.

More complex, however, is the task of processing information. Processing, before we transmit and after we receive messages, determines what meanings we will assign to words and other symbols of language. And meaning is critical to understanding.

How accurately meaning is conveyed depends on the thinking (intellect) and feeling (emotion) mechanisms we all possess. We'll label this the *thinking process*, and explain why later.

Our ability to anticipate, observe, record, evaluate, and respond combines with our five senses to provide us with a totally integrated communication system. This system acquires inputs from reading (seeing), listening (hearing), nonverbal communications (facial expressions, gestures, etc.), and the remaining senses, touching, smelling, and tasting. It transmits outputs via writing, speaking and nonverbal communications. Inputs and outputs stimulate and drive the process. However, it's thinking which binds the forms into a system.

Regardless of the mode in which the system may be operating —internally (*intra*-personal communications) or externally

(*inter*-personal communications)—it does not move on separate acts alone. On the contrary, it incorporates those acts (sensory, verbal, or non-verbal information) and runs them through a myriad of gates and filters associated with instinct, intellect, emotion, and experience before arriving at some reaction or response. This may occur rapidly (often instantly), or it may require some time. In either event, what is operating is a process which thinking makes possible.

Each person comes to the party with his own operational system. This system may be impaired or otherwise constrained by physical damage, emotional disruption, or intellectual deficiency—but it exists, nonetheless. However, let's just consider those people who pass for normal (whatever normal is).

Another person's system is never precisely the same as yours, nor is it ever exactly attuned to yours. Your respective systems will never process inputs in exactly the same way. Occasionally you'll reach similar conclusions after processing the same inputs, provided intellect, logic, training, and experience are the primary processing factors. But when emotion intervenes you'll rarely get similar responses and almost never identical reactions—even to identical inputs.

Emotionalism

Intellect and emotion obviously are not the same thing. However, they do function in a common environment—the brain and other aspects of the nervous system—and they do account for, or are in some way involved in, all human behavior. So allied in performance are intellect and emotion that one may mask the other, making it difficult to detect where one stops and the other begins in a person's reactions and responses to messages. Moreover, since we tend to express thoughts and feelings the same way—usually through verbalization—it's not uncommon for the terms to be used interchangeably.

People will tell you "This is what I think" when what they mean is "This is what I feel." What they may be expressing is a reaction to some input, albeit one for which they've yet to develop a logical response. Or perhaps it's just an imprecise use of language.

On the other hand, people sometimes say "I feel this way about that," when what they mean is "Here are my thoughts." This response may be, and often is, logically based, and the person may have little or no emotional reaction to the material under discussion.

As a communicator, one of your toughest jobs is to separate emotional from intellectual responses to your communications. Most resistance to your directives, advice, and ideas is emotionally based. Even when resistance is rationalized, seeming intellectual and logical, you'll find some emotional rejection of your position lurking in the background.

You'll find it, that is, if you look for it.

Intellectual resistance to or rejection of your communications may lead to emotionalism—on your part or another person's. However, emotional resistance, as soon as it arises, interferes with a person's receptivity to a message. Almost immediately he reacts and begins preparing his response. This virtually shuts down the communication process, at least temporarily.

For our purposes we may consider that the process through which messages are accepted, resisted, or rejected is called *thinking*, since the process begins or ends with intellect or at some level involves it. And since emotions are usually expressed in an intellectual way, the problem of acceptance becomes quite complicated. There are three reasons for this: (1) Emotions can be difficult to uncover and deal with, (2) they are the chief impediments to communication, and (3) they are usually the *real reasons* behind resistance to and rejection of your communications.

Establishing a Communicating Relationship

Once you're certain (as best you can be) that your message has been clearly transmitted; once it's apparent that your words have been understood by another person, you can be sure only that the communication process between you has been stimulated. *You cannot be sure that you and the other person have communicated*.

Not until the other person responds or reacts in some way can you determine the operating condition of the process you're mutually involved in. His reply may be agreement or acceptance, resistance or rejection; but whatever form it takes, unless you understand the real reason for it, you and he are not truly communicating. In the case of resistance and rejection, you'll find—if you dig—that the more deeply a person is entrenched in his position, the more emotion is embedded in his response.

Knowing this in no way gives you license to shrug off resistance with "Oh, he's just being emotional." Such a response is itself emotional—and self-defeating. Since you must live with your employes and other personal and professional associates, you must deal with their personalities, their individuality. If you don't need others to do your job and to enhance the quality of your life, you can afford to discard them at the first sign of disagreement. And if you feel this way, hopefully you can also afford the services of a good psychiatrist.

Most of us, however, can't afford either to give up human contact or go to a psychiatrist. For us, the positive alternative is to cope with people—ourselves and others—and the situations we all create. To do this we must observe, contemplate, and evaluate behavior, our own as well as that of others. The goal: to maximize our understanding of how communication systems and the communication process operate. In short, we must think about how these function and why we fail.

You can apply this knowledge of individual commonalities and systemic differences to great advantage—if you're willing to do the hard work required. Consider these suggestions:

1. Before attempting to communicate with another person, particularly on some important matter, find out "where his head is"—the condition and operating mode of his processing system at the time you want to communicate with him.
2. Try, as best you can, to attune your respective systems. A couple of questions or a few introductory remarks may either do the job or get things started in the right direction.
3. If your previous attempts at communication with the person have been unsuccessful, he may be resisting. It's also possible that you failed on your side, that you were unclear in articulating your position. It's easy and not uncommon for us to confuse talking with saying something. Before you verbally assault the person or abandon further attempts at communication with him, find out the problem: Is it him, or you?
4. If the problem is his resistance, try to determine the *real reason* for it. This is often as difficult as it is necessary. But there's no alternative if you're going to communicate with him.

5. Having done all this, consider his position, reevaluate your own, and try again. Reconsidering and adjusting your position in light of new information—the other person's views—is not the same as copping out.

When you successfully apply this approach, the result is to get two independent systems to perform cooperatively. You create what amounts to a new, common process which can facilitate communication between you and the other person. This new process amounts to a *relationship*.

By discovering the real reasons for another person's resistance, by adjusting your positions where necessary and where possible, by accommodating his views and feelings, and by allowing him to see and otherwise sense these changes via your responses, you can remove certain ego-threats from his perception of you and your views.

In the work place, supervisors and their employes have opportunities to develop nonthreatening, mutually rewarding relationships. These can be quite conducive to individual and corporate health. They are akin to what in our personal life we call *meaningful* relationships. Supervisors who attain such relationships with employes are said to practice "positive human relations." True. But it's done through communication.

Knowledge and awareness are not synonyms, although they are occasionally used interchangeably. Much knowledge we acquire and file away; sometimes forgetting that we possess it. Awareness means *to be conscious* of something. In the connotative sense, awareness comes closer to alertness than to knowledge. It's this meaning that advances our understanding of communication.

We pay much lip service to individuality. Almost anyone you meet can make a fine and pious-sounding speech on the subject, extolling the virtues of personality differences, marveling at man's distinctiveness within nature. Blah, blah. Yet when we must deal with each other, when we must communicate, we seldom carry our knowledge forward into actions which reflect *awareness*.

Mere acknowledgement of differences between people is insufficient. A successful communicator remains aware, alert to matters both overt and subtle which either drive or impede the communication process.

Terms such as "system" and "process" may seem spooky because of their association with technical pursuits. They are two of the most overused and abused words in contemporary parlance, being used so often and to mean so many things that they hardly mean anything at all without great explanation.

Back to Basics

In its simplest form, a system is nothing more than a combination of two or more components, or parts, joined in an orderly way to accomplish some purpose. A razor is a system. A lamp is a system. A car is a system. A space satellite is a system. We are systems.

A process is a means of getting from here to there. Whenever two or more functions are performed in series to achieve a given goal, you have a process.

When your communication system and that of another person attempt to achieve understanding between you, you have a process involving three functions. What's going on between you (your respective words and actions) is only one-third of the process. The most important parts, the other two-thirds, are what's going on inside you and what's occurring inside him.

Each person's communication system is constantly and simultaneously performing numerous functions *at multiple levels of awareness*. A veritable bombardment of sensory stimuli competes with every message you send to another person. If you fail to get his attention, you will obviously fail to communicate with him. Getting attention is tough enough. Holding it can be even more difficult.

Attention, like respect, generally must be earned if it is to be maintained. Extraordinary events and circumstances can gain attention, but interest holds it. What are people usually most interested in? Themselves. How do you hold their attention? Get to know them. Operate with an awareness of their interests as well as your own. Put another way: in your communications make their interests your interests. It's called "knowing your audience."

Subtleties in System and Process

A conscious communicator acts with an awareness that:

- Each person in his audience functions through a uniquely individual communication system.
- Each person's interests, aspirations, experiences, perceptions, and skill in using communications tools varies widely.
- Sensory stimuli can be competitive as well as supportive in the communication process, making maintenance of audience attention difficult under the best of circumstances.

If you lose awareness that thinking, as defined, drives the human communication system and permeates the entire interpersonal communication process, then you create the worst of circumstances. Neglect the subtleties of the system and the process and you obscure the obvious. To illustrate: Two people begin with a disagreement and end with a hassle. During the encounter they articulate their respective views in a clear, well-organized manner. Each gives the appearance of listening to the other's points. Sounds like a pretty good argument. But they conclude further apart than when they began. Why?

Since it's been stipulated that each person presented his argument in some appropriate way, the answer must lie in the transition—the conversion of output to input, the processing, the assignment of meaning to words. What appears to have been clear output from one person enters the communication system of the other and becomes input. It's processed through the gates and filters of individual psychology. Some material passes smoothly, some gets altered, some is trapped. The result may or may not be communication. For instance, the parties may agree to disagree. If they do, provided they understand the *real reasons* for each other's disagreement, they have communicated.

We've probably all witnessed scenes in which two people strongly disagreed. The harder one tried to convert the other, the further they drew apart. The more emotional the discussion became, the more the dissenter resisted. The advocate's arguments may have seemed lucid and reasonable to a bystander, but obviously not so to the person he was trying to convince. This is another view of the process in action. It reveals the individual distinctiveness of people as communication systems—processing the same material but arriving at different conclusions.

The preceding is only one example of two people confronting each other and attempting to use communication as a bridge across individuality. It illustrates the routine, not the extreme. It's vital that supervisors of people discern and deal with these individual system dynamics if communication within our organizations is to occur in other than a catch-as-catch-can manner—too often the case at present.

Too often our response to resistance is not to pause and recall what we know about people and the communication process. Rather, like the advocate in the argument, we continue a communications bombardment which further entrenches people in their resistance. In the case of communications, *more* is not always *better*, and sometimes the acts negate the desired result.

Sensing the Process

Quite frequently we feel a requirement for visual contact with another person with whom we want to communicate on some important matter. At such times we may say, "This is something we'd better discuss in person. I'd rather not talk about it over the phone." And such conversations were occurring long before wire-tapping became a national sport.

Why do we occasionally feel the need for visual contact? Certainly not because telephones *per se* impair our ability to speak or hear. However, the absence of visual contact does negate our ability to "hear" with our eyes and to "talk" with our hands, among other things. In sensitive or otherwise important matters for discussion, we want every faculty, every component of our communication system available. We want and occasionally need this because alternatively our system must operate with imcomplete information.

When we're unable to see the other person we feel constrained to mere words. From his voice tone, inflections and selection of words, we may or may not detect his interest, concern, sincerity, and other emotionally related responses. Nor can we always be certain that ours are getting through. In most circumstances the combination of visual and verbal contact removes this barrier. It permits our communication system to operate at optimum efficiency.

Visual contact enables us to verbalize such things as facial expressions: what we see we identify as interest or lack of interest, concern or apathy, getting through or getting nowhere, and so forth. Of course, we sometimes see what we want to see and hear what we want to hear, but that's a different phenomenon and one that can be overcome by exercising objectivity regarding oneself and others.

The better our relationship with the other person, the less important the lack of visual contact. Obviously, the better we know the other person, the better we can imagine his expressions and gestures. And the more confident we are that the relationship itself will overcome semantic difficulties. But it won't always.

Even in the closest, most intimate relationships there are often times when nothing short of being in each other's presence —the sharing of space, and visual as well as verbal contact—will do. At such times, our communication system clearly shows that it operates through a process.

Debugging the System

The word "system" implies that a thing works, although harried commuters, accustomed to coping with something called a "transportation system," may dispute this contention. And of course they're not alone. Most of us have heard "system" applied to all sorts of practices, procedures, and operations which appear to require more effort to achieve less efficiency. In truth, many so-called systems are nothing more than a collection of unrelated activities slapped together for organizational convenience rather than structured to attain some semblance of efficient performance.

Here's a clue: If you carefully study something labeled "system" without discerning the functional relationship between the components and between the system itself and the work to be done, more than likely what you're looking at is a *potpourri*, not a system.

Even the best systems occasionally fail if people fail to maintain them properly. This is true with communication too. In fact, it's the failure here which brings about breakdowns in other systems and functions. Sometimes, however, the failures occur because we lose sight of just how efficiently individual communication systems operate, and because we mistakenly act as if the communication process were linear.

As it happens, our individual systems sometimes work so well that they impede or impair the very process that we're trying to achieve. Success, in this case, results in failure.

Neither our system nor the process operates in a straight-line fashion. Therefore, we must occasionally restrain the system if the process is to function properly. Consider these points on the nonlinearity of both system and process:

1. We continue to think while writing and speaking. These activities actually lead to further thought. The quantity and quality of our thinking probably correlates with the amount of effort and the degree of care we exert in word selection and other factors which affect the cogency of our presentations.
2. It's obviously possible for us to listen and write and to listen and read at the same time. Again, this is made possible by thinking, which coordinates the effort and converts distinct and otherwise unrelated activities into a process. Furthermore, there are people who can speak and listen, if not precisely at the same time, then close enough to it to enable them to participate in more than one conversation simultaneously.
3. We can also hear without listening; see, touch, and smell without learning from the experience; write without purpose, talk without really saying anything. These are all variations of doodling. They indicate that the system is operating, but they're distractions from the communication process.
4. Each of us is constantly gathering information from multiple sources, but we sometimes forget that others are doing the same. Thus, when you prepare a letter or report, for example, the process may appear linear in that you gather information, analyze and evaluate it, organize your material, prepare the document, edit it, perhaps have it typed, edit again (hopefully), and transmit. However, since you don't transmit

into an intellectual, perceptual, emotional, or experiential vacuum, it's likely that certain members of your audience already have some knowledge of the document's subject.

5. Such readers may also have opinions on the subject —opinions other than those expressed in your letter or report. Others in the audience may lack prior knowledge, but they may have feelings aroused by what they read. The basis for their feelings is already there. Your document merely stimulates them. Emotional reactions may join intellectual opinions held by your audience.
6. It's also possible, even likely, that someone receiving your document will have more knowledge of the subject matter than you do. In that event, despite the fact that such a person sits and reads your document, his communication system, like those of the others mentioned, will be operating at a level of awareness different from yours.
7. Even your own activity in generating the document doesn't follow a straight line from mental effort to mail room. Once you begin the preparation process you don't stop thinking, nor do you necessarily stop gathering inputs. More often than not, if you approach the job conscientiously, you'll modify your document for one reason or another throughout the preparation process.

Communications involving and affecting every person in your various audiences are going on all the time. These compete with your communications for people's attention. The more people who comprise an audience, the more difficult it is to attain communication with them. There's almost no way to determine with certainty the phase in which an individual's communication system is operating when he receives some message from you. With a group, the determination is impossible. But the situation is not hopeless.

Being aware of these phenomena is a form of preparation. Your awareness should alert you to every opportunity to narrow differences and reinforce points of commonality between you and the people in your audiences. The job is demanding and often frustrating. However, you can overcome competing stimuli, and gain and hold audience attention.

By planning and presenting your communications in ways which reflect your own awareness of the existence and nature of interferences, and by showing an understanding of individual human differences, you can acquire respect for your communications and for yourself as a communicator.

Chapter 5

Talking Back Is Not Back Talk

Defining Terms

Communication between two people occurs through a process. This process links three distinct and dynamic functions: the transmitter's thinking, the receiver's thinking, and the media each uses to convey and achieve meaning. Media is the plural of medium; a medium is a go-between. In the communication process, any medium will do, so long as it facilitates the transfer of meaning from one mind to another.

Communications and media are synonymous for our purposes. Any action, device or method used to stimulate one or more of our five senses, arouse our thinking center, and make us receptive to a message qualifies as a medium. Each of the three functions, though independent, must operate compatibly with the others if the process is to work at all. A failure in only one function disrupts the entire process.

The terms "transmitter" and "receiver" are intended only to aid your visualization of the process. However, there's probably no time when a person operates exclusively as one or the other. We're all transmitting and receiving simultaneously, constantly.

Even when we're talking—transmitting—we're receiving and processing new inputs at the same time. We "read" facial ex-

pressions, gestures, and other indicators of audience attention and reaction to our words. When writing—actually another form of talking—we attempt to anticipate questions and imagine audience responses as we prepare our document.

During discussions we not only receive nonverbal communications from others while we ourselves are transmitting verbally, we also plan our subsequent comments (think ahead). Usually, we can see with our mind's eye the conclusion of whatever message we're trying to convey to others. Furthermore, we're constantly receiving and processing sensory signals emanating from the environment and from within ourselves. These, of course, are potential distractions.

Our internal (intrapersonal) communication system continues to send and receive messages even while we're involved in the external (interpersonal) communication process. Put another way, our sensing of surrounding stimuli and our processing of these stimuli, which provides us with meaning, does not stop when we begin to talk or write. Our thought process never ceases.

Turn it around. Imagine yourself on the listening end. Assume the role of receiver. Though your mouth may be silent or your pencil still, your mind is active. It sometimes shouts, sometimes whispers your responses to spoken or written communications—while those communications are in progress. This also occurs when you're reading. Reading is another form of listening. There's no beginning, no end to the intrapersonal communication process; no time when we're exclusively the transmitter or the receiver. And this creates some problems for us.

Anticipation and Distortion

Our intrapersonal system never shuts down. It's constantly sending and receiving messages, processing data from external and internal sources. Small wonder, then, that another person's attempt to convey some message rarely, if ever, gets our undivided attention. His message represents only one input entering our system. It arrives concurrently with a myriad of other stimuli; joins all those inputs which are already in the system; competes with our thoughts which have nothing to do with his message.

That should be trouble enough. But there's more.

As noted earlier, while a person is trying to convey some message to us, we're often busy anticipating, rebutting, or otherwise passing judgment on his message—before the entire message has been transmitted. Sometimes our communication system works too well for our own good. However, this isn't the last of the problems.

Unlike even the most sophisticated computing machines, our individual communication systems needn't await the arrival of inputs before designing solutions, reaching conclusions, generating responses. There's always plenty of data in the system: attitudes, knowledge, opinions, prejudices, hang-ups. All there, waiting to flow forth.

Solutions may be incorrect, conclusions inaccurate, responses precipitous; but that's no deterrent. The system—we—will act anyhow. When we lack information, the system makes up its own. This applies with people as individuals and in groups.

Employe group process produces organizational "rumor mills." When employes lack sufficient or credible information from their management, they generate their own versions of the way things are or the way they ought to be. Call it flights of fantasy, ridicule it as wish-fulfillment—but don't ignore it. Unchecked rumors are dangerous to corporate health.

These human characteristics create distortion factors. And distortion factors, coupled with the way we handle language, are among our principal problems in communication.

In our highly verbal society, sensory inputs are translated into words, and words comprise the majority of our communications output. "Seeing" is tantamount to listening with our eyes. What we see, we label. Reading causes the thinking function to evoke within us mental images of the things symbolized by words. In the first case, what we see we label; in the second, what's already labeled, we see.

Our tactile and olfactory senses provide us with still other devices for listening. Through thinking, we assign verbal meaning to sensations experienced via touch and smell.

The meanings we attach to sensory experiences we express symbolically, mostly through words. In order to relate experience, describe thought or emotion, we rely on words or on gestures which others will interpret as words. When these vehicles succeed in transfering meaning from one mind to another, communication occurs. If the transfer does not occur, there is no communication.

As it happens, we're often inept in our choice and use of words. Our thoughts are imprecise, our communications incomplete or inaccurate. Meaning is not clear. On these occasions, the link between communication systems—people—is not formed. Such failures impede the process by distorting our perceptions of other people and their views. One person's inadequate or inappropriate use of words may arouse conflicts—intellectual or emotional—within another person's thought process. The result: no understanding; no communication.

If the parties attempting to communicate do not align their individual systems (their thinking) so as to form a channel through which communication can flow, or if the words and other symbols they employ to express their thoughts fail to convey the intended meanings, communication between the parties does not occur.

Closing the Loop

The three functions—thinking on both sides and the symbols used to move messages—must be treated as inseparable, almost as a single function, in order for the communication process to operate. Contrast this with the nature of communications.

Communications are devices, forms, media through which we attempt to achieve communication with one another. They are conveyors of words, conduits for thoughts. They are the vehicles on which messages travel.

Communications initiate the movement, exchange, or transfer of ideas, information and other communication system inputs between people. They can stimulate the interpersonal communication process, but they are not the finished product. This is why, having written or spoken, we cannot content ourselves

that we have communicated with another person. Activities such as writing and speaking merely get things going—open the bidding, so to speak.

Most communications are substitutes for direct contact. Their intended role is to transfer material from one mind to another, but without the parties actually discussing the message together. Thus a movie maker, painter, or writer may say through his medium: "This is what I see, think, or feel. Do you see, think, or feel the same thing?" If your answer is yes, then you two have communicated.

But something may still be missing. The experience often does not give complete satisfaction. The transmitter and receiver usually cannot be certain that they communicated. (How many times have you discussed with friends a movie which you've all seen, only to discover that you've all gotten at least a slightly different message from it?) Furthermore, the receiver, although his involvement is essential to completing the process, frequently feels no sense of contribution, no linkage with the sender.

The communication constantly going on inside us requires an outlet. However, most communications we encounter afford us little or no opportunity to engage the people who prepare them. We often must externalize the feelings and thoughts which communications arouse by discussing them with third parties. This can be frustrating business. It also can impede the communication process.

Consider some communications with which you routinely come in contact: memos, letters, reports; books, newspapers, magazines; paintings, photographs, billboards, posters; highway directional and safety signs, traffic lights; package labels and product use instructions; radio, recordings, TV, movies. All of these have their place and contributive value. And all have something in common: incompleteness.

These media reveal thinking and expression of thought on one side only. Using them as their vehicle, people send messages *at* or *to* other people. However, those on the receiving end usually have no immediate method available by which they can seek clarification of a point or question the sender on what they see or hear. Resistance to or rejection of the message must usually be discussed with a third party. Consequently, the vital third function of the communication process is suppressed. When the opportunity for exchange is removed, the *with* function is missing.

Whenever a person's participation in the process is restricted to interpreting, the likelihood that communication will occur is restricted. We may see or hear a message, but if we can only

evaluate its meaning internally, rather than discuss its nuances, or perhaps even add to it, we're likely to be less interested in completing the process than might otherwise be the case. This is true in organization communications as well as artistic endeavors.

On the other hand, when people can talk back to communications the way is open for them to participate more fully in the communication process. The higher the level of participation, the greater the chances that communication between one person and another will occur.

Here's To You, Mr. McLuhan

All people who pass for normal have some need to communicate. This doesn't mean merely "to talk." It means to participate, be part of the events that affect their lives and destinies. When a person participates in the communication process, he senses not only that his words are heard but that he, as a person, is listened to. This participation, this feeling of being part of something vital, contributes handsomely to a person's self-esteem.

There are times when we're all unsure, both of ourselves and of the motives and messages of others. We seek confidence, clarification. When we contribute, we reassure ourselves and others of our worth.

Communications often put us in contact with things when what we need is some relationship with other people. Through relationship we acquire the opportunity to share in the communication process. We derive meaning from the experience of participating as well as from the symbols exchanged. One medium maximizes participation, and that medium is conversation. All other media are surrogates of conversation. This is not to say that they have no personality, engender no conviviality. However, all communications except conversation are limited and incomplete, constrained as they are by format. Conversation, particularly in-person conversation, has no format. It goes where we take it; it shifts, adjusts, inquires, responds as our needs require and our desires point us.

As our technology makes available increasingly more sophisticated means of exchanging information, people are removed further from the process. We become to a greater extent gatherers of data, receptors of transmissions. But this is not in our nature. We want the benefits of technology—and rightfully so—but we don't want to be dropped from the process.

This need to participate often conflicts with the paternalism exhibited by our organizations. And it poses other problems associated with our societal profit orientation. For our employers, communicating *at* everybody is cheaper and less time-consuming than communicating *with* somebody. It's also less effective, but many organization managers don't seem bothered by this fact.

Not so with employes. Many feel not so much *left* out as *shut* out of organizational affairs. Again, this brings them into conflict with their organizations. More importantly, it doesn't set with

their self-concept. Since the need to communicate is a strong one, and since the need is best fulfilled through participation, denial of the opportunity to participate amounts to a suppression of the need. When prolonged, this may be perceived as the denial of a person's existence. Thus the charges regarding dehumanization mentioned in the Prologue. And paternalism, which infantalizes people, treats employes as children, is tantamount to a denial of their existence as adults. Hardly a tolerable situation despite its apparent prevalence.

Advances in communications technology touch every aspect of our lives. To be uninformed or uninvolved today, you almost have to try. Our media make us involved whether or not we want to be. No longer must we wait to learn about change. We witness it. While this is informative and often interesting, it's also frustrating—even frightening to many people.

These emotions may arise from an impression that major, sometimes drastic, decisions affecting our lives are made and implemented so quickly that we have no recourse but to follow along. Support change or get swept away by it. But we occasionally wonder if anyone's in charge. Are people shaping events? Or are events occurring so rapidly that they dictate our behavior?

But psychologically, this won't do. These questions promote insecurity, which for the sake of self-concept must be dealt with. Enough remoteness. Enough of the illusion of intimacy. Enough reactive participation. Bring back people!

This is a mounting plea among the citizens of our organizations as well as those of society at large. It cannot be ignored because it will not go away. Nor should it.

It seems that Marshall McLuhan was right: the new technology does raise its predecessor to the level of art form. Perhaps conversation was not precisely what he had in mind, but the principle applies.

As our gadgets continue to ease the burden of labor and speed the flow of information, more and more people come to value conversation as if it were an art form. Where once we merely used it as a means of getting things done, today it's associated with satisfaction of the items heading our hierarchy of needs. Relationships are more important to job satisfaction than even money. Check it out with your firm's resident shrink or management consultant. See for yourself. A sense of participation gives people a feeling of contribution and, to some extent, control. Conversation provides an escape from the desperation imposed by the perennial question mark. It evokes the satisfaction implied in the exclamation point: I am here! I am participating! I am important! I *am*!

Today, much conversation takes the form of confrontation. This can be counterproductive, since confrontation often raises more issues than it settles. Confrontation may alter behavior, and thus the relationship between parties. However, since confrontation implies intimidation, it's usually only the *behavior* that changes. More often than not, the prevailing *attitudes* are reinforced.

Confrontation does have its place. It's an outlet, a recourse, a battering ram applied to the walls of inertia. Yet, in a civilized society, why should so much confrontation be necessary? Could it be that tomorrow we must not only get organized but civilized as well?

The Shoemaker's Children

Conversation, including that between an employe and his employer, is potentially the most gratifying form of communication. Remove threat, fear, and deceit; eliminate the euphemisms which we substitute for candor; call off all the game-playing —and the opportunity for a genuine relationship surfaces, becomes unobscured. Discussion makes people answerable to each other. Unfortunately, this is precisely what too many of us, as senior executives, as supervisors, as people, want to avoid. Conversely, and paradoxically, we all want to participate, feel involved and important, live and work with fewer problems. However, while we demand these things for ourselves, we often deny them to others. It seems like a contradiction of our stated desire to participate. One can hardly participate alone. (Actually one can. But the activity involved still doesn't have high social standing.)

The reality is that we often want to be followed, be the high-muck-a-muck, but without exhibiting any qualities of leadership. And many of us want all this without sacrifice. Forget it.

As an alternative to conversation with our employes, we can continue our heavy reliance on other, less personal communications: forms, memos, letters, spoken direct orders, employe publications, and all the other escape routes from meaningful contact. These do keep employes in their place—outside the organization's communications process. But we'd be better advised to take one lesson from our counterparts in the communications industry, those organizations which comprise what's known as The Media.

Media executives have precisely the same problems we do. Why shouldn't they? They deal with precisely the same audience: people. Furthermore, since the majority of American adults work for organizations, it's obvious that these same adults, also known as employes, buy most of the magazines, newspapers, and products advertised on TV and radio. Same audience.

Differences arise, however, when we compare the approach media managers use with their audience (i.e., almost everyone's employes) with that taken by other business managers when dealing with their employe audience. Those in the media appear to understand their audience.

While organizations generally are accused of impersonalization, of ignoring the human need for participation, and of reducing the opportunities for it, media managers are striving to make greater opportunities available. Many media managers seem tuned-in to the shortcomings of their own media.

People remain involved with media provided they understand what's going on, are entertained, or are otherwise getting something out of their reading, listening, or viewing experience. However, when understanding or appreciation cease, media become remote rather than personal. Media officials deal with this reality.

Under the worst of circumstances, radio, TV, newspapers, magazines—the mass media—are no more remote or impersonal than a letter from your senior executive addressed "to all employes." Such a letter certainly qualifies as a mass medium.

How do you talk back to a letter from your organization's president? How do you respond to your radio or TV? In the first case, you probably wouldn't, even if you agreed with his views. Too many up-tight little people occupying positions between you and the top person might be frightened by your initiative.

Knowing that you could be ostracized, your career possibly jeopardized should your message skirt the chain of command, it's more likely that you'd make your comments to a third party. But in the second case, radio or TV, not only is there no threat, there's opportunity. Vehicles are available and your comments are welcome.

The electronic media follow an example set by the print media. They not only welcome your comments, they've initiated talk shows on which numerous people who are presumed to have something topical to say discuss their views with other individuals on the air—in person and occasionally in living color. There are many phone-in shows as well. And, thanks to the FCC, there's more public service programming than there used to be, more opportunity for citizens to be heard. You can even respond to a station's editorial views. The print media have their own tradition of encouraging and publishing letters to the editor. Many columnists also reprint their mail.

Both print and electronic media provide all manner of audience assistance and citizen services. Many radio and TV stations offer prizes and publicity to people who phone in news tips. This isn't a means of getting more news at no cost. Responsible media officials spend money to verify the accuracy of information so received. So what's the gimmick? What are they after?

Involvement. Participation. Retention of interest.

Despite some opinions to the contrary, America is not yet a nation of voyeurs, more interested in vicarious participation than in activity itself. Not content to watch from the sidelines, most of us want an occasional turn in the arena. The media are providing that opportunity. Letters to the editor, talk shows and all the rest provide an outlet for people's viewpoints. They address a psychological need which, admittedly, is coincident to the media managers' primary mission—the holding of audience interest and loyalty in order to attract and retain advertising revenue. But they do make participation possible.

These are, of course, commercial moves made for profit, t› please customers—your employes, as well as program sponsors

Your organization probably has similar ventures directed toward retention of customer goodwill. But what about employes?

Innovations in employe relations tend to lag behind creative steps in customer relations. One wonders, for instance, if media executives encourage employe involvement in corporate affairs with the same fervor evident in their efforts to retain public interest. Or is it another case of the shoemaker's children going without shoes?

Employes Want to Participate

Priorities differ with each audience. Employes have seen their rating, and many don't care for it. More employes are growing dissatisfied with their receiver role. Nationally, employe expressions of frustration and resistance to one-way communications appear in what for corporate America are revolutionary ways: diminished craftsmanship, increased quality control problems, demands for more money with less work, earlier retirement. Again one wonders: If work were more satisfying, perhaps even enjoyable, might not more people prefer to spend more time doing a good job, rather than less time doing just enough to remain on the payroll?

Not that the vehicles of participation are unavailable. *Organization* implies participation by numerous people in the pursuit of a common goal. The means to provide it are readily available. Devices such as suggestion plans, roundtable and staff meetings, and man-manager conversations afford employes some opportunity to participate as initiators of action. But too often expectations, which we arouse, exceed results, which we produce.

For instance, where employe suggestions, submitted through either a formal plan or in an informal way, are ignored, unacknowledged, or arbitrarily rejected, employes themselves may feel rejected, disenfranchised. Where meetings with managers serve only as platforms from which we hurl additional instructions, admonitions, and slogans at employes, their perception that we regard them as mere objects is reinforced. Under such circumstances, more communications bring fewer positive results. They broaden the relationship gap.

The term "mass communications" makes us think of radio, TV, newspapers and magazines. Perhaps books and movies too. The term has a big sound. But how big is a mass? That question is in a class with how high is up?

Keep in mind that intraoffice or interplant memos, letters "to all employes," training films, the employe newspaper (to name just enough to give you a hint), are all mass communications. And all have the same drawbacks: You can't be sure anyone gets any message, let alone that everyone gets the same message.

But there are even greater hazards. These arise from the way people may eventually respond to impersonal communications. Apathy and indifference are passive responses. Resistance and rejection are active responses. Don't confuse *no* response with a negative response. They're different. In each instance, however, the receiver does not continue the action or process set in motion by the sender. He initiates his own process. He may do this for a number of reasons, among them: disinterest in the subject matter; failure to understand the material; failure to discern that a response is expected of him; hostility toward the sender. The list goes on.

Whatever the reasons, it seems clear that when we, as receivers, lack a sense of participation in the process, when we feel constrained to the role of receptor, we perceive no risk or loss should we not get the message, should we not react to it, should we reject its content.

Even in serious matters we're quite capable of rationalizing these feelings. So are our employes. To many of them, it seems that only occasionally can they sense a stake in communications; even less frequently, that they can influence the communication process—or us.

The best of communications only pinch-hit for conversation. They build bridges between people's thinking, which is accomplishment enough. However, without involvement and participation by the people on both sides of the process, the bridge stands on sand because it rests on formality.

And life is a very informal place to be in.

Chapter 6

A Personal Approach to Personnel Relations

The Communication Climate

Everyone is familiar with the term *work environment*. We think of it as a place, the setting in which we work. But it's more than a physical location. The work environment is also a *feeling*.

Ask a person about his work environment and he may say it's noisy, needs paint, has lots of light. Obviously, he's referring to the physical surroundings. But don't be surprised if instead he replies in terms which reveal his feelings toward his boss, his work group, the organization itself. He's commenting on the work environment, but he's describing the *communication climate*.

Every organization has its unique communication climate. Climatic conditions are influenced by managers, employes, and external sources such as customers, competitors, and government. But managers usually have the greatest impact on the communication climate. They can make it tolerable, comfortable, or oppressive, depending on their behavior. However, your decisions in this regard should be made carefully and consciously.

The climate in which you attempt to communicate predetermines to a large extent your success as a communicator. It is often more influential than the material contained in your message. For these reasons, it's useful for organization officials to create a climate which as closely as possible approximates the conditions encountered in conversation.

Mass communications are of course essential to the dissemination of information within organizations, and are especially crucial to the operations of large, diversified, or geographically dispersed organizations. We must employ methods which will enhance the effects of such devices, but we won't succeed in this by continuing to mistake the action for the results.

Since communications are conversations (albeit often remote ones) between senders and receivers, we have a starting point. And since organizations place people in a more-or-less common setting and provide the basis for relationships (for better or for worse) we now have three starting points in our favor. What shall we do with this knowledge?

Let's hold it aside just for now and consider what else we know. We know that conversation stimulates more sensory involvement, and arouses greater participation than most other communications experiences. (I've deliberately excluded sex.) We know that in-person conversation, which adds the dimension of *presence*, is preferable and usually more rewarding than other forms. We also know that most human beings have a need for some sort of productive endeavor. Furthermore, we have in our possession a body of knowledge which we often ignore, but which tells us that all people have needs (not desires—*needs*) associated with the maintenance of self-concept and self-esteem. And finally, for the moment, we know that when people have positive feelings about their organizations, their management and associates, their jobs—and thus their role in their organizations—they are more apt to have positive feelings about themselves. This also works in reverse, when the vibrations are negative. In either event, one will reinforce or otherwise affect the other.

Positive feelings make for healthy relationships. Negative feelings create adversary positions. Where the relationship be-

FIGHT TEAM FIGHT!
GO TEAM GO!!

tween employes and their organization is positive, where they perceive the relationship as mutually rewarding, they have good feelings. As one result, they can often take even bad news in stride without losing faith and trust. Where they perceive the relationship as exploitative on the organization's side, the vibes are bad and won't be easily converted. No amount of "Go-Go!" "Fight Team Fight!" cheerleading from faceless, incredible sources will correct the situation. More often they will reinforce the negative feelings, since once again the possibility for dialogue and self-expression has been precluded.

What this says is: people communicate with other people, not with things. The definition of a healthy communication climate therefore seems obvious.

- It enables people to form positive relationships—within themselves and with others.
- It allows them to participate in the communication process, not merely serve as targets for executive missives and the drivel disguised as information by so many so-called employe publications.
- It permits them to believe much of what they hear from managers and act accordingly.
- It brings them in frequent contact with those who influence their economic—and to some degree, emotional—rewards.
- It fosters a sense of satisfaction engendered by dialogue, the feeling of belonging, contributing, participating.

In such an environment, communications in all their forms, have an excellent chance for success. They can help to achieve communication.

Here, however, irony casts a cloud over so many organizational environments, chilling the climate and precluding the very communication officials claim to seek. Without question, the major contributors to communication climate setting are the *first-line* supervisors. And who are they? Generally the most harried, most time-pressed, most ignored, least informed, least trained for human relations, least influential members of management in the entire organization. All they do is supervise the vast majority of employes.

Isn't that astounding!

Toward the Nitty-Gritty

Small wonder communications so often fail to result in the communication intended.

Communications are only devices, tools. Like many implements, they are versatile; one tool may serve numerous purposes. But just as you don't say that you own a house because you possess a hammer, you can't conclude that you've communicated with another person simply because you've spoken to him—or at him.

Communications are problem-solving tools. They are not themselves problem-solvers. People create problems, people must fix them. And the so-called Communication Problem is an event, not a diagnosis, despite our propensity to pretend the latter. Communication doesn't fail people, people fail to communicate with one another.

Some confusion arises from our definitions of communication. These, too, can reveal our priorities. Ask some people how they define communication and they'll probably describe how they use *communications*. Communication is a very personal thing. It means different things to different people, depending on their priorities at the time you solicit a definition. Thus a universal definition may be impossible. It may be immaterial, as well, for the point is that we're usually thinking of one thing while we're describing another.

Communication has been described as:

- the discussion of ideas or information
- the transmission of viewpoints, instructions, or requests
- the transfer of knowledge from one person to another

- the expression of opinions or emotions
- a way of gaining acceptance, altering behavior, or motivating people
- shared thinking

There are other descriptions, but these are representative. However, while each of these activities may result in communication, only the last one—shared thinking—strongly implies that we actually get there; that meaning moves between people; that understanding occurs. The other descriptions content themselves with communications (acts), stopping short of the vital end result: communication.

Seldom will your inquiries bring responses such as: "I employ communications to acquire information; to find out what people are thinking or feeling; to determine whether I should do what they want." Rather, most often it goes the other way: "*I* am the almighty disseminator."

We've now journeyed from some relatively restricted descriptions of communications to an expanded perspective of what communication is all about, how it functions. A progressive step.

That's why a definition seems immaterial. Definitions by their nature are restrictive. They can cause us to infer, often erroneously: This is what a thing is and everything else is something else. Just the result we want to avoid here. Ideally, if we can abandon some of our misconceived notions about communication, its nature and function, we may never again have to hear the strident sound of our own voice crying, "We're not communicating!"—when we know damn right well what we mean is: "You're not doing what I want you to do!"

Climate-Setting: Opening Corridors

Return for a moment to "shared thinking." What's implied here is not that people have identical thoughts or mental processes, but that they occasionally stand on common ground, figura-

tively speaking. This comes closest to communication and to what our organizational goal ought to be.

A dictionary entry refers to communication in terms that are more physical than mental, but which nonetheless aptly suit our purpose. The reference is to *connecting passages* or *corridors* joining one place with another. This is precisely what communication between people amounts to: a linking up of minds, thought processes; the construction of connecting passages between people through which messages and their meaning may be conveyed, unencumbered, undistorted. In short: understanding.

There's a fallacy, frequently found in our management practices, that understanding, agreement, and acceptance are the same thing. But how can this be?

- A person may agree with your position without fully understanding it.

- He may disagree in ignorance.
- He may accept your position and perform in accordance with your directive without either agreeing or understanding. He may do this if he has faith in you, if he's apathetic toward the situation, or if he's coerced into obedience.
- He may understand your position and its consequences better than you do. If he dislikes you, he may not question or try to help you; rather he may feign acceptance or agreement, knowing that you will be harmed in some way as a result —which, of course, he'll rationalize as your own stupid fault.
- He may accept your position, even agree with it, but take no action if he fails to understand that action is called for. The result: it appears as though he did not agree or accept, and this further confounds understanding between you.

While acceptance, which often is passive rather than active, and agreement, which often is obtained through threat and the withholding or withdrawing of rewards, may masquarade as understanding, they are not synonymous. Conversely, people may understand each other's positions, yet withhold acceptance and agreement. This often occurs in labor-management contract negotiations. In these, as well as more personal negotiations, people may pretend not to understand—or they may occasionally deny understanding in the face of reality. Self-interest is both a great motivator and a distorter of communication.

Unfortunately, in organization life, acceptance and agreement attract too much attention, acquiring disproportionate emphasis. The goal seems to be to effect the greatest behavioral response with the least amount of effort. However, the goal defeats itself and frustrates the organization's members.

Establishing understanding between people is costly, time-consuming, and difficult work. In financial and psychic terms, however, it is much less expensive than the alternative.

We tend to question what we don't understand, not only because we're inherently curious, but because we distrust—and thus challenge—those who presumably possess information of importance to us without sharing it. Mutual understanding—of organizational roles and responsibilities, and of individual expectations—engenders respect and faith. Both are related to credibility.

And it's credibility that keeps the communication corridors open, that keeps the process free of the serious distortions which can preclude understanding and, thus, communication itself.

Time and energy devoted to climate-setting, which encompasses all the activities associated with the treatment of employes *as people*, is more an asset than an expenditure—and one which appreciates rather than depreciates. A climate which is conducive to communication, where understanding is encouraged and fear minimized, justifies the expense of such things as employe publications, large-scale meetings, and the occasional hoopla associated with the employe communications program. But these things are wasted, are often counter-productive in a climate characterized by doubt, uncertainty, incredulity, or oppressiveness.

Where employes perceive selfishness as the hallmark of the organization's operations (and this impression they get from supervisors as well as top management people), resentment and rejection of management messages are a likely result. In such cases understanding occurs, albeit in a perverse way: the organization is a lousy place in which to work, and employes understand that it is. Since institutional spokesman lack credibility, their communications are seen or heard, but unheeded. Right on, employes!

On the other hand, where employe/management relationships have more of the aspect of partnership, communications from management elicit greater interest and concern, enhance the relationship, and increase the potential for communication.

Communication, once the corridors are open, is easier to sustain than to establish; immeasurably easier to sustain than to reestablish. Where the climate is healthy, where relationships are understood, where they are perceived as mutually reward-

ing, supervisors can spend more time on planning, production, and performance evaluation and less on petty crises which never should have arisen in the first place. On the other hand, communications conceived in crisis are usually still-born.

No improvement, however, will occur until we show a better appreciation, a fuller understanding of the communication process. If and when we begin to act on what we know about people and the processes through which they function, communications will lead more frequently to communication. But not before.

Those things which management determines are in the organization's best interest are not always perceived by employes as in their own best interest. And in the absence of a truly positive relationship, why should they be? Communications from management usually express the organization's (management's) interests. Such communications commonly reflect management's assumptions of what employe interests are, or should be. Management may assume erroneously more often than not, at least with regard to employes' real interest, since employes may feel only a landlord/tenant relationship with their employers.

A healthy communication climate gives people contact, a sense of connection with the organization. It provides a feeling of participation in the organization's and one's own destiny. It enables even formal and printed communications to attain some of the results of conversation. Where the climate is healthy, where faith, trust, and consideration prevail, a nod is as good as a missive. Sometimes better. Conversely, where the climate lacks these factors, no amount of missives will make it better.

Communications provide us tools with which we can create a climate for understanding. They offer us a means through which we can build quality relationships and in so doing enhance the quality of life—individual and organizational. However, they are only tools, useful and necessary to the process, but implements nonetheless.

Communication occurs through a highly personalized process and is itself such a process, now synthesizing, now separating in never-ending operations. It is sensing, feeling, thinking in a ceaseless drive to achieve understanding.

When meaning is detected, digested, understood, then, and only then, does communication occur.

Communication occurs as an individual event because it issues from a personal understanding, an individual response, not a mass act.* To understand the communication process, its function and dynamic forces, is to understand people—oneself and others, our commonalities and differences—and why we so frequently fail as communicators.

---

* Chapter 15 describes a program for Creating a Climate for Understanding.

Part Two

ORGANIZATION CLIMATE: MYSTERIES, MYTHS, AND MODELS

Chapter 7

Mysteries

In the Beginning . . .

Everyone is born a communicator. So in a sense we all start even. From earliest childhood we learn what behavior will be rewarded, what will be punished, what will be ignored. Somewhere between Pablum and puberty we fine-tune our technique. We improve our ability to discriminate between those words and actions which bring positive responses (those we want) and negative responses (those we want to avoid). This learning occurs through communication.

Adolescence is an arbitrary status assigned the young by nature. It's a period of searching and uncertainty. Learning stimulates curiosity—a little knowledge demands more. And as we sharpen our communication skills, our questions become more incisive, more probing. We no longer accept a blunt "because" as a response to "why?"

We discover irony. On the one hand, certain questions considered sensitive by our elders are answered with "You're too young for that," or "You'll learn all about that later," or "There's plenty of time for that—when you grow up you'll understand." On the other hand, we're occasionally admonished to "Grow up," "Show some responsibility," or, "Act like an adult—you almost are one." What more nebulous status than "almost" an adult?

But at the time, we think we know. So we emulate adult behavior, sometimes without realizing it, sometimes believing we're actually rebelling. Adult approbation is a formidable, though elusive, driving force.

We earn praise, not always knowing why. We discern that silence is often a reward, the absence of criticism a signal of success. We learn because we are communicators.

Finally, adulthood arrives. Freedom. We escape adolescence and enter the world of work. But then a mysterious thing happens. The cycle, with all its ironies, is repeated. Freedom repealed.

Regressive Organizations

In terms of their communication practices most organizations probably are regressive. They place adults in adolescent situations. And the more authoritarian the style of an organization's top managers, the greater the tendency among lower-echelon managers to infantilize their employes.

There's an inherent danger in such behavior. Put briefly, where employes are afraid to ask questions, they're usually reluctant to make suggestions. Obviously little or no dialogue between adults is possible in such a setting.

In an organization where the chief rule for survival is "Don't ask questions, just do as you're told," or worse yet, "Do exactly as you're told and maybe you won't get fired. . . today," you'll find employes who are most treated like children. After a while (not surprisingly) that's the way they'll perform.

In some ways not much has changed over the last few thousand years. Families expanded into tribes and contemporary organizations are fashioned after tribes, subdivided into families. This makes today's supervisor an authority figure somewhat like a family head or chieftain of a small tribe. That's a heavy responsibility and a marvelous opportunity. However, if your supervisory method is "management by mouth," expect to encounter with your employes many of the same problems you might incur with your teenage child. And much of the same behavior, too.

Management by Mouth

The "management by mouth" style characterizes the most insecure supervisor. He may adopt it for numerous reasons:

- He may be unsure of his own future with the organization.
- He may be uncertain of his own role, knowledge, or leadership ability. Perhaps he's insecure in all three categories.
- He may be uncomfortable in the relationship he has with his boss.

All of these are unhealthy for the supervisor, his employes and the organization.

If you attempt to dominate every discussion with your employes, if you almost always tell people what to do and almost never ask their opinions on how to do the job better, if you threaten rather than encourage your employes, you're managing by mouth.

If suggestions from others, including employes, make you angry and defensive (because you didn't have the idea yourself?), if criticism from your boss causes you to cast blame on your employes, if even small mistakes drive you to berate your employes, you're in trouble. You're also in the wrong line of work.

Evolution has taught us that people are most adaptive creatures. They generally adjust to their surroundings and circumstances. However, when they do so to survive within a poor organizational environment, you can be sure that it's for their own protection and welfare, and not for the benefit of the supervisor or the institution.

Such adaptive behavior takes many forms. People perform their duties to the letter of their instructions. They don't look for better ways, and when in doubt, they stop working on an assignment until they can locate their supervisor, get new instructions, or have a question answered.

This accomplishes many purposes: It takes the employe off the hook for any errors; it creates more work for the supervisor; it enables the employe to mask his lack of enthusiasm as conscientiousness.

Supervisors who demand letter-of-the-law performance from their employes often get it. However, like the intractable father, they don't always enjoy the result.

> As junior returned home one day, a bag of groceries tucked under his arm, he announced: "Hey, Dad! I just saw a guy steal your golf clubs out of the car." "What are you doing here? Why didn't you chase after him?" demanded the irate father. "But gee, Dad," said the wily youngster, "you told

me to go to the store and come straight home. And you always say I'm to do *exactly* as I'm told."

The boy was obviously on safe ground, while his father mired in quicksand of his own making.

People in authority can easily become impressed with themselves, their status, and their power to dominate the will of others. However, many supervisors and parents eventually learn the hard way that obedience and respect are not the same thing. You may demand one, but you must always earn the other.

Discipline is a requisite for order in any social body, ranging from one person to society at large. People require some sense of order or structure in both their professional and personal lives. Whatever its label—ethics, standard of conduct, law, or work rules—discipline is the fabric from which a society is woven.

Unfortunately, it's as easy to confuse discipline with what in the military service we called "chicken shit" as it is to mistake authority for leadership. Authority is bestowed and may be removed by others. A boss is a boss as long as he remains in power. Leadership, on the other hand, carries authority but does not depend on it. Leadership cannot be taken away by others; a leader is a leader as long as he chooses to be, even though people may cease to follow him.

Authority pushes. Leadership gets people to push themselves.

Authoritarians, the practitioners of "chicken shit," are often intellectually deficient and emotionally immature. Being incapable of maintaining employe interest via meaningful assignments, and fearing that inactivity will lead to mutiny, some make up rules and regulations to which they then demand strict adherence. This creates an illusion of efficiency. However, not only does it fail to produce anything of value, it weakens the relationship between boss and employe.

Such supervisors may be threatened by the job, the boss, or others in the organization. But in truth it's mostly their own discomfort with a leadership role that causes the problem. Unsure of themselves, they distrust others. Of course, they may not be consciously aware of this behavior, and, if confronted, they would probably deny the charge vehemently.

Look around your own organization. How many leaders can you identify? How many autocrats? How do you rate?

It's a tough test, mostly because you're probably not as familiar with your associates' management styles as you should be. Usually we're so busy with our own jobs and our own work groups that we don't take the time to discover what's going on elsewhere. That's one of the major communication problems organizations incur.

If you take some time, however, you'll learn quickly that work groups that are led by their supervisor are open in their communications and cooperative with others. You'll also observe good rapport between the supervisor and his people and among the employes themselves. Conversely, work groups that are driven by some unenlightened dolt tend to be closed and uncooperative. They're as noticeably deficient in communication as their supervisor is in leadership. Employes in such groups become survival-oriented; they're concerned for their jobs but not the business. Gossip, bitching, and "beat the boss" games evoke the best intragroup communication. Consequently, when organizational goals are met, it's almost by accident.

Desperate employes can always beat the system and the supervisor. If enough join in a unified and subtle effort, they can depose a despised supervisor. For obvious economic reasons, top managers almost always replace an ineffective lower-level manager rather than fire an entire work group.

Not surprisingly, most of us check in somewhere between the leader and the loser. We possess characteristics of each. We also have options: We can let our own goals, expectations, and anxieties blind us to the humanity of others, or we can pursue the path of leadership. We do have a choice.

Management by Ear

Contrast "management by mouth" with "management by ear."

Anatomically, the ear is an organ which catches and relays sound to the brain. In concert with the brain, the ear acts as a sensing device. It can detect a multitude of words in almost infinite combinations. Of course it's the brain that analyzes those words for meaning, emotional content, attitudes, etc., but the ear is the conduit, and that's an important role. The ear takes in. The mouth gives off (mostly hot air, in the physical and metaphorical sense). Little learning is acquired through the mouth.

Supervisors who manage by ear not only talk to their employes, they listen to them as well. They're interested in employes' views. They encourage suggestions and solicit opinions. They're tuned in to their employes' aspirations and ambitions, alert to their needs as humans.

Such supervisors are eager and able to interact with others at all organizational levels. Being sensitive and *feeling* people themselves, they understand the humanity of others. This empathy enables them to cope with the multiplicity of personalities and problems which pervade organizational life. Other things they are not. They are not easily threatened, and they are not insecure regarding their own position and capabilities.

Maybe it's maturity. It's also smart management.

It's smart management for a number of reasons, all of which benefit the organization and its employes.

One reason: Few employes are content with the role of hod carrier, placidly hauling stones to their supervisor's altar of success. While they may think him worthy of promotion or other recognition, they usually want to experience success themselves. Everyone seeks his own version of job satisfaction. The savvy supervisor knows that his employes work *with* him, but *for* themselves.

Another reason: Most employes will behave as adults if given the opportunity. This leaves the supervisor time to cope with the relatively few children in his organization. Since the adults, if properly trained in their jobs, can perform some self-management, the supervisor can devote more of his energy to vital duties such as planning and the maintenance of peer and upper-management interfaces crucial to his performance and career. Put another way, he can do more useful work and eliminate much unnecessary hassle from his life.

And still another reason: The supervisor who communicates *with* rather than *at* his employes engenders a spirit of mutual respect within the work group. People must come to know one another before they can understand and respect one another. By avoiding the authoritarian approach to communication (which evokes hardly any communication at all), and by allowing employes the dignity of their adulthood, the supervisor-leader stimulates rather than stifles the employes' sense of responsibility. The rewards of this are evident in the job performance of a work group so supervised.

Message for Bargain Hunters

All businesses evaluate their financial status periodically. A key item of such reviews is "return on investment." Unfortunately, however, there's no report line labeled "return on *human* investment." Considering the costs of recruiting, hiring, training, paying, and providing benefits to employes (which are the major costs to a business) it certainly would be instructive for managers and investors alike if there were an effective measurement of employe utilization.

As it is, there are alleged measurements of "cost effectiveness." However, we often confuse this concept with "cost control," and they're definitely not the same thing.

You can control costs by curtailing purchases; buying inferior tools, supplies, and materials; and by furloughing employes. Or you can lay off your high-salaried people and retain those at lower wage levels. In which case you may harm the future of your business. Another game is to use high-level people to do lower-level work—and lay off the bottom-echelon employes. This helps to control costs, but can also work to destroy morale if played too long.

"Cost effectiveness" must address "the effect of costs" on a firm's financial condition; management's effectiveness as spenders of corporate resources. The term implies the pursuit of optimum value for each dollar spent. Since employe costs —payroll and others—generally account for more than half of a firm's cost of doing business, it seems logical that a supervisor who best helps employes rise to their maximum contributive capacity best serves the business as well as the employes themselves.

Doing the job cheaply is not always the most efficient way. If good management were merely a matter of cost control the supervisor's job would be easy. It would also be empty. People pose our challenges and only through people can we earn rewards.

Maximizing employe potential requires trust—trust in employes to act responsibly, though with guidance, and trust in yourself, your own capacity to cope with the reality that being a boss does not make you infallible. Your employes will make mistakes which will occasionally cause you grief. So will you. Work together. Learn together.

The message is this: People occasionally fail—sometimes in spite of their best efforts, sometimes because of their worst. It's human. It happens. It generally can be corrected. In order to succeed a person must have the opportunity to fail. Just as important, because we may not make it the first time, a person should have a chance to try again. Only by overcoming adversity, including failure, can we ever truly succeed.

How much is enough? How much responsibility can your individual employes handle? How many failures is each one entitled to? That depends—on you, on them, on the circumstances surrounding each individual, each case.

Your work group is a collection of individuals brought together to achieve an organizational objective. Each person is unique, yet in some ways the same as others. You've got to grasp the thread of commonality while you seek to unlock the mysteries of individuality.

You'll find your answers neither in the authoritarian nor the permissive management style. Permissiveness is a pit for the unwary, a pothole on the road to respect and success. Many a nice-guy supervisor has been returned to the ranks or drummed out of the corps because his employes liked him without respecting him. Somewhere between the tyrant and the "taffy" stands the humane supervisor.

Consider for a moment: Where do *you* stand?

Center Stage

It's madness to isolate a person's job as a supervisor from his role as a communicator. Whether or not a supervisor sees himself as a communicator, others do: his employes, his peers, his boss.

The supervisor is the focal point of communication within his work group. Furthermore, he's involved in the process of moving messages up, down, and across the larger organization. Where a supervisor succeeds in this switching-center capacity, people in his own group operate more efficiently and those in other components cooperate more readily on matters of mutual interest. As a bonus, upper management may even be more responsive to his requests and suggestions.

Within his own group, the supervisor/communicator has an even more crucial role: that of climate setter. He must manage his employes' and his own behavior in such a way that a climate for communication is created and maintained. Where the climate is comfortable, people will perform their duties and cooperate with each other with relative ease. On the other hand, where there's excessive stress—caused by fear, uncertainty, or distrust—you'll find only the *appearance* of communication. People may work at their jobs, but they won't willingly extend themselves for others or the organization. In short, a selfish supervisor portrays the entire organization as selfish and employes generally respond accordingly: they look out for themselves.

Closing Skill Gaps

Although people are born communicators, and despite the fact that most have the basic tools of the trade, few have much skill by the time they begin their careers. Many employes, particularly those in numerous clerical and so-called blue-collar occupations, are discouraged from communication excellence by family or peers. The process operates as a kind of reverse snobbery which inhibits learning by stigmatizing educated people. This, in turn, can cause a severe self-concept problem for a person. On the one hand, he may desire education; on the other he may be threatened by education, knowing that achieving it will separate him from his family and friends. The relationship between him and them, he supposes, will never be quite the same because of his educational advantage. More times than not he's correct. The situation is slowly improving, but it's still a problem.

For many people, perhaps most who have these conflicting feelings, the price seems too great. So they avoid it, thus preserving their family and peer relationships. Unfortunately, in too many cases, they pay a penalty for this choice later in life. When that time arrives and such people join your organization, you'll share their self-imposed burden. You'll work extra hard at communicating with them and at teaching them to communicate skillfully with others. You will be compelled to do this by the certain knowledge that they lack the initiative and training to do it for themselves.

Other employes will come to you better educated, perhaps, but similarly lacking in communication skills. They will have attended a high school, or even college; however, as communicators they may be little more skilled and no less a burden than those just described.

Our educational system seemingly resists change. It has been lambasted, its end-product lamented by people across the spectrum of professions because, it's said, the system simply does not teach people to communicate. Furthermore, the argument goes, for what we pay for the system—as individuals and as a society—we deserve better.

Students are often fed facts but not encouraged to learn. Some teachers evidently believe that education must be disguised—turned into a game—in order to be acceptable to kids. This failure to interest, arouse, and excite the young with the possibility of what Edith Hamilton called *the joy of being an educated person*, we call progress. Somehow that seems a peculiar label when so many products of the system emerge unable to read, add and subtract in their head, write a lucid sentence, or even speak their own language properly. Many students, even on advanced levels, acquire technical knowledge but little understanding of its applicability to their lives and career pursuits. How many acquire diplomas or degrees but little or no education?

As it happens, however, we may not be getting what we're paying for but we're probably getting what we're asking for.*

Nor are teachers alone. They are part of a society in which parents too frequently cop out and expect the system (any system) to do the parental job. Schools do not replace parents; parents must supplement, and in many cases, foster, even lead, the educational process. And let's not discount TV with its persistent programming appeal to the lowest common denominator of audience. All these factors are important. All are a piece of the problem.

Organizations dominate America. Traditionally, the educational system's role has been to fill the labor pipeline, provide the personnel needed by our corporations and other organizations. When measured against the international monetary standard of living and our Gross National Product, it appears the educators have done a pretty fair job. So what's the complaint?

Just this: The educational system prepares many people for jobs but relatively few for life in a complex society. But why should that be surprising? Why should those who control organizational life, and who have made a near-science of placing people in little niches and occupational boxes from which escape is often difficult and occasionally impossible—for both economic and emotional reasons—why should they complain when their pipeline pumps out just the product they ordered?

Perhaps the educators are confused. And why not? Why should they be different from the rest of us?

What becomes of all those "bright, dynamic innovators," those "aggressive, creative go-getters," those "no-nonsense self-starters," those "leaders" who get the jobs heralded by the

---

* I don't believe there is anything planned or deliberate about all this. What concerns me is the lack of what in engineering might be called a forcing function—some pressure to improve the product, in this case. I believe further that educators are no less intelligent or conscientious than other professionals in efforts to improve both their profession and the product. What I argue with is the result to date.

LABOR
PIPELINE

classified ads? Not uncommonly, one of two things: They adapt, conform to the corporate mold, or they become the next generation of "trouble-makers," "malcontents" and "poor team players."

Curiously, in baseball, for instance, a person who hits .350 isn't merely an asset, he's a treasure. He may also be regarded as a great team player. Take Joe Dimaggio—and who wouldn't have? Compare this situation to what we may encounter in our organizations, where the .225 hitter—the mediocrity—is often more to management's liking.

The innovator, the leader, the "tiger" is the person everyone wants in the classified ads and almost no one wants in the plant. Or so it would seem. And the message, though subliminal, evidently is not lost on the educators.

Agreed: Educators are not supposed to be order clerks. Each has an honorable occupation, but their functions differ—or should. Organizations, and especially business organizations, create both the supply and the demand—protestations to the contrary. If our behavior, which includes the way we utilize people, demands mediocrity, the educational system will produce such a product. But when we get just what we've ordered, we shouldn't complain, nor should we be mystified by the product's performance.

In a related issue, our insistence on college degrees for even clerks, our propensity for comtemporary mythology ("You've got to have a degree to get ahead."), and our preoccupation with what amounts to institutional status-seeking have accelerated the demands on the academic side of education and dramatically decelerated attention to the vocational side. This has wrought numerous additional human problems for supervisors to cope with.

Roles and Relationships

Most profound of these problems is a sort of organizationally induced inferiority complex not uncommon among tradesmen, craftsmen and other "blue collar" workers. Their condition —and your job—can be aggravated by the educational elitists who inhabit many organizations, and who may have influence in yours. Their power, their advantage, often rests on the appearance of superiority. This may come from merely being a member of management or from possession of certain academic credentials. But curiously, some of the same people, with a string of letters after their name, are incapable of properly putting one word after another in a letter or report. We must be doing something wrong.

Somehow we must get this message across to all people throughout our organizations:

- A manager or supervisor, whatever his title, is just another employe. He plays a distinct role. He usually bears greater responsibility for the actions and decisions of the organization and as such should be entitled to certain rewards. But

he's not a king to be served by the serfs, who themselves have no rights and privileges except those gratuitously granted by the manager.

- So-called professional people: lawyers, accountants, engineers, others, have their roles too. But they're still employes. Roles and rewards fluctuate in importance and nature depending on the needs of the organization. This is as it should be.
- Other employes, ranging from custodians to clerks to craftsmen, also have important organizational roles—otherwise they shouldn't be on the payroll. These roles, like the others, vary in significance, skill requirements, and organizational worth. However, in human terms—needs for recognition, reward, self-esteem—they're no different from others. At a given point in the manufacturing process, a first-class machinist is worth any number of engineers. At certain times in the economic cycle, the worth of a journeyman craftsman far exceeds that of a manager—or writer, for that matter. Why, then, should we persist in affording these employes only second-class citizenship within our organizations?

We pay an exorbitant price for our disregard of what motivates people. Starting with the many mental drill sergeants who pose as teachers and culminating with autocratic managers who deny adults the opportunity to act the part, we create and maintain successive generations of intellectual invalids—and continue to wonder why.

Chapter 8

Myths

Myths frequently acquire the force of truth, even when they lack the prerequisite of fact. The notion that certain races of people are inherently inferior to others gives rise to numerous myths.

Mythology pervades history, art, religion, politics. On occasion, it even creeps into science. Myths flower also in the field of business.

When we employ myths as allegory or to make a moral point, they serve a useful purpose. However, when we rely on them to justify our prejudices, or as a substitute for reason, they have a highly adverse effect.

Some myths are impervious to reason and logic, springing as they do from emotional rather than intellectual origins. They virtually defy intellectual assault.

A fact provides evidence from which an intellectual conclusion may be drawn. Myths often represent conclusions which ignore evidence and resist reason. These may be defended by orderly, seemingly logical arguments. However, such arguments can disguise the real reasons for the persistence of myths: emotion.

If people want a situation to be a certain way, if they wish it hard enough and repeatedly rationalize their views in public, they can gain acceptance for their argument from other people who hold similar prejudices. When this occurs, a myth is born.

Some myths impede social justice, causing their adherents to violate at least the spirit of civil rights laws. They foster discrimination against certain people. Other myths imperil employe/management relationships. These don't encourage discrimination against any employes. They foster discrimination against all employes. Brotherhood at last!

Three factors make the myths we'll consider here most vexing:

1. They're born of apprehension and mistrust. As such, they engender more of the same.
2. They're rarely, if ever, discussed openly within the work place. Here's an unusual situation—where keeping our mouths *shut* gets us in trouble. The trouble, in this case, is conflict between people who ought to be cooperating with one another.
3. Uncritical, and indeed unwitting, acceptance of these myths leads to attitudes and then behavioral patterns which, themselves, go unexamined.

The sum of these three factors is mythology in action.

Senior executives are among the chief mythologists. They set the pattern and provide the model for management behavior throughout their organization. They represent the success stories. Thus, we reason, they must be doing something right. However, we—and they—often forget that as practicing human beings, they're not perfect.

Many top managers embrace some peculiar attitudes which they don't express in public. Since these attitudes aren't discussed with employes, they can be only indirectly challenged. But they remain entrenched. Let's dig them out and see if we can deal with them.

It's unlikely that a senior executive would inform an audience of his subordinate managers that he thinks they're something less than competent. He certainly would berate them regarding

their role in a given corporate set-back, but we're dealing with something different here. We're talking about a continuing attitude of condescension.

Myth No. 1

Superiors are always smarter and more competent than their subordinates.

The real problems arise from the attitudes launched by this myth. For instance, it's a short and frequently taken step from thinking you're smarter than someone else to believing that he's not very smart at all. The same applies to competence and other matters affecting performance in the work place. You can easily see how the road to infantilization is paved.

There's usually lots of ego-defense involved here. This need reinforces the attitudes springing from Myth No. 1 and sets up Myth No. 2.

Only the rarest of senior executives will stand up and tell his subordinates that he, personally, is emotionally threatened by their initiative, ambitions, and skill. He might gig a peer or two, but that's not very common either. In truth, the executive probably shouldn't make such an admission. However, organizations would be healthier if more top managers would 'fess up to themselves. Instead, we have more mythology, intended, no doubt, to keep subordinates and seniors in their respective places for as long as possible.

Myth No. 2

Only the top people in an organization have any genuine commitment. Most, if not all the rest are only in it for the money and other selfish rewards.

To paraphrase an old adage, everybody's ripping off the system but thee and me—and I'm not so sure about thee.

From this perspective, it's easier to see clearly the reasons behind so much senior executive skepticism regarding subordinate competence. There's also a little popularized paranoia here. Furthermore, some folks always feel bigger when they're putting others down. And if they feel big enough to carry the weight of an entire organization—with just a little help from a few friends—they can bear even to be put-upon.

And what better way to impede the progress of an ambitious subordinate who poses a threat to your position than to spread the word through the senior ranks that he lacks initiative, management maturity or skills, or commitment to the honor and glory of the organization?*

---

* The preceding are, of course, generalities. They represent conclusions drawn from 15 years in business and four in the U.S. Air Force. As regards these attitudes, I didn't find any appreciable difference between the two entities.

Generalities can be misleading. Treating them somewhat facetiously raises the risks. But the points are serious ones. Even those managers who ardently defend employe rights, and who work diligently to overcome their own fears and ego-threats, tend not to rely much on man-

For those who skipped the footnote: These generalities reflect real attitudes—attitudes which influence behavior in your organization today. Don't be too quick to shout Right On! because you're inferring from all this a frontal assault on your senior management. They're acting out the preceding illustrations all right, but so are you. And that's the real message.

Actually, there are two messages:

1. While we're busy evaluating the performance of other managers, we still must take time to rethink our own attitudes and behavior. (Whose promotion did you impede or simply shoot-down lately? Why? The *real* reasons.)
2. Senior managers are the most visible people in an organization. Even when they're inaccessible, they are still the main, though symbolic, targets of our discontent. Many times they deserve it. But they also merit a bit of compassion.

The pressure of senior-level responsibility may be real or imagined, but it's always a factor in organization mythology. People can be trained in the technical aspects of management, yet the burden of ultimate accountability causes many to stumble and some to collapse under the weight. Symptomatically, this may be manifested as mistrust of the motives and competence of others.

There's still no fool-proof method for preparing a person psychologically for management at any level. There's no way to guarantee that he will be able to handle a string of pressure-packed assignments successfully. Nor is it certain that even a successful manager will not one day succumb to the rigors of responsibility.

---

agement subordinate and other employe competence. I've found little faith in employe commitment to the organization, and almost no expectation that most people will perform in other than a mediocre fashion.

Turns out, these are increasingly accurate perceptions. But one wonders: whose chicken produced what egg?

Not all people, including top managers, feel pressure the same way; nor do we all deal with our roles and responsibilities in identical fashion. Some people prepare themselves admirably for the job. Others may arrive at the top as if by accident. The best managers of people (rather than managers of paper) are prepared by virtue of the relationships they've developed within the organization. Consequently, they know the capabilities and personal characteristics of the people they must rely on.

Mostly, though, you prepare yourself by getting to know yourself.

Regardless of his rank—first-line supervisor or senior executive—the manager who is unsure of himself will be unsure and probably suspicious of his employes. He may be intelligent, competent, and confident in technical matters, yet uncertain of his standing with his boss and uncomfortable with his responsibility as a manager. The ambivalence regarding his position can mislead him in matters involving allocation, utilization, and understanding of human resources.

Myths One and Two create adversary relationships within the work force. Top management attitudes relegate subordinate managers to a despised role: that of outsider. But it doesn't stop there. There's a trickle-down effect. Subordinate managers, in an unconscious effort to regain some self-esteem, replicate their superiors' attitudes and behavior in dealings with their own subordinates. Guess who gets shut out? Right—the people at the end of the line. The people who produce the product. The employes. Myth No. 3 illustrates the procedure.

Myth No. 3

The higher a person's organization rank, the more information he requires to do his job; also the more he can be trusted to handle sensitive information discretely—in the best interest of the organization.

This is partially true—the part about requiring greater amounts of information. The part about handling sensitive information is true to the extent that having all the facts of a situation and knowing their implications does equip a person for discretion. However, it's also true that some of the biggest blabbermouths and some of the least trustworthy individuals in an organization are found at the upper echelon.

The obverse implication here is that the *lower* you go in the organization, the *less* people should know and the *less* they can be trusted to behave in the organization's best interest. Small wonder, then, that so little accurate or useful information filters down through the ranks. This is especially true of bad news, which is commonly clouded by so many euphemisms and outright distortions that a disaster looks like a major victory. Yet for some reason, we seem puzzled—and highly critical—because employes lack commitment.

When top managers behave as though lower-echelon employes don't know the difference between excrement and useful information they delude only themselves.

Employes have their own sources, their own information system, separate from the management channels. These usually carry the news ahead of communications from management. Not that the employe network is flawless. Far from it. That system transmits information indiscriminately. Fragments. Rumors. Gossip. It may not always operate in the best interests of the organization, but it does provide a check-point when management fantasies are disguised as information. Furthermore, it enables employes to participate in the communication process, and it fills their need for information which at least seems to come from a credible source: another employe.

The less an organization (management) talks with its employes, the more they talk with one another. In the long run, this can be detrimental to the organization. Information flowing through the employe network may differ drastically from a story disseminated through the management channels. Who to believe?

More employes know what's going on in their organization than management people realize. The problem is, they generally know less than they should. However, the mailboy delivers more than mail; the shop worker has friends in the various offices; secretaries may appear to hear no evil, see no evil, but speaking about what they hear and see is often another matter. And why not? In this regard how are employes any different from management people?

Consider again the reporting of bad news. By the time management comments on some issue, numerous employes already know what happened. They've got a fairly good handle on who did or did not do what to bring about some adverse event. And they've already told others. Consequently, when official communications attempt to obscure the facts, if not deny outright that any setback occurred, few people may be fooled. But management's credibility surely will be diminished.

Following a campaign of supposedly inspirational hoopla, during which employes are implored to exert the wholehearted, dedicated effort required to capture the vital such-and-such contract, the announcement of the contract's loss to a competitor (if there is any announcement) may be clothed in so many cliches that the reason for and meaning of the loss are themselves lost.

Sometimes, it's difficult to determine if there was a setback at all. Such communications often imply: "We lost this one, gang; but the next one is the one we *really* wanted. *This* one didn't mean that much." Of course, the communique never says it in those words, but presumably that's what employes are supposed to believe. "Forget what we said before—that was yesterday. Now that we're through the warm up, we're ready for the *big* game!"

How employes are to be ready for the next game, not having learned anything from the last one, is a mystery. Why so many managers opt to bury "lessons learned" rather than share them with the employes, is another mystery. The notion that employes (and first-line supervisors usually are included here) are insufficiently mature to handle at least the approximate truth about events which affect their lives, is an insidious myth.

It sometimes seems that the only contracts lost were those management didn't want to win anyhow. The stiff-upper-lip facade is commendable, but when it's maintained as a fiction and employed as an alternative to telling the children (the employes) what's really going on, no one learns anything for use in the next round of competition.

Employes know there can be no victory without defeat. And there are still some left who want to believe that management is doing the best job it's capable of. Put another way, employes are potential allies, not the natural enemy of executives. We all help to create the combatant roles.

And there are still employes who want a hand in shaping their own destiny and that of the organization. However, to do this, they must have useful information from which they can learn, correct mistakes, feel more a part of the organization's efforts.

Obviously, not everyone needs all the details of every situation in order to do his job or to feel a part of the organization. The indiscriminate transmission of information, which usually leads to misinterpretation, can harm the organization whether it's transmitted by employes or management. Supervisors must exercise judgment, but they too must get sufficient accurate information from upper management in order to judge properly.

The deliberate distortion of information, predicated on the myth that only a small elite has any right to or need for accurate information can destroy management's credibility with employes. Eventually, this loss adversely affects productivity and profitability.

When credible information is unavailable from management, employes will turn to other sources. They'll spend time exchanging gossip, rumors, and complaints, and in a sense pondering their roles and futures with the organization. In the meantime, little or no useful work gets done. How much money is lost through this otherwise unnecessary activity?

Once dissipated, management credibility is almost impossible to regain with the same management people. Only the most narrow, unenlightened managers blame employes exclusively when this situation arises.

The myth may be more comfortable for a few people, but the reality is more rewarding for the organization.

Myth No. 4

People get paid to do what they're told to do. Consequently, the only information they require are instructions and directives on assignments to be performed. By restricting information flow, by operating in an atmosphere of secrecy, not only is there less chance of a compromise of organizational security, there will be a greater tendency toward organizational order. The more employes know, the more they'll want to know. Eventually, this will cause them to question management decisions—and that's not conducive to good order either. When managers feel compelled to answer questions relating to decisions, directives, and operating procedures, a diminution of discipline ensues, since employes will come to believe they have a right to know.

This myth has much in common with Myth Three. However, this one thrives where managers lack confidence in themselves and in other managers, rather than in employes. It signals insecurity and easy susceptibility to ego-threat.

Where senior managers rely on authority of position rather than the authority of knowledge, supervisors encounter much difficulty in acquiring useful information for dissemination to employes. Such an environment usually contains a great deal of antipathy and conflict between management and employes.

There are, of course, many occasions when secrecy must be maintained. Crucial contract negotiations and periods of planning to outwit competitors are just two examples. This is true in business and in government. However, some business organizations tend to follow the distressing and faulty model developed by certain government agencies—they "classify" everything.

The fallacy of this behavior is evident both in employe (or citizen) loss of respect for such organizations, and in people's refusal to accept such institutional practices. It's now clear that, attitudinally, when everything is secret, nothing is secret. People will make up their own rules. They will follow their own course of conscience, rather than accept and incorporate seemingly irrational practices as a way of life.

Contrary to the beliefs of some managers, secrecy only fosters the need for more secrecy. It does not breed order and discipline. It does not generate feelings of loyalty. People are loyal to other people and to ideals. Relationships rely on integrity. They thrive on communication. Remove these, and you plant the seeds of revolution.

Revolution need not be violent. And it may be quite subtle. Revolution begins with a change in attitude. In the work place, this change may cause employes to reject management's demands and practices. Work rules may be ignored, production may be slowed, employe complaints requiring upper-management attention may increase. In short, lost credibility and employe refusal to accept cavalier treatment can conspire to bring about the very disorder and turmoil which management seeks to avoid.

Order and discipline are functions of faith—in oneself and in others. But faith requires feeding. In organizational life, nourishment comes from positive relationships and a flow of credible information. Senior managers and supervisors who cannot accept this and act accordingly are clearly unsuited to their jobs in the social environment of the 70's.

The sweat-shop management mentality, if not dead, is at least expiring gradually. What's needed now are managers and supervisors who can tell the difference between proprietary information, the release of which might adversely affect the entity and employes alike, and information which employes require to satisfy their need to participate and enhance their job performance.

As supervisors, we should know our employes well enough so that we recognize what information they *should* have and what information they *feel* they should have. Both are important. Too often, we make our decisions in the vacuum of ignorance, without understanding employe needs and aspirations. Consequently, management communications often contain information which employes already possess, have little use for, or care nothing about.

In short, it's imperative that supervisors and other management people who want employes to care about the organization, not merely about themselves, give employes something to care about *other* than themselves.

When a person perceives that his presence makes a difference and that his destiny is somehow intertwined with the organization's, it's more likely that he'll seek ways to maximize his contribution. He may then manifest greater fidelity and be more willing to accept the judgments of knowledgeable superiors. This kind of relationship between employes and management—this climate for communication—improves order and increases productivity. Conversely, authoritarian secrecy precludes a positive relationship and diverts management attention and energy from the pursuit of organization objectives.

Myth No. 5

Management achieves communication with employes through articles in the employe newspaper, executive speeches, letters, memos and reports, policy guides and work rule handbooks, and the instructions issued by supervisors.

Here's a classic employe communications program—one-way, from management to employes. Either directly or by implication, such communications tell employes what management wants done. However, they don't feed back to management the employes' questions, concerns, or complaints. The mechanism for inquiry is missing.

Employes, like all people, require outlets for their thoughts and feelings. And they find them. So don't arbitrarily assume that the relative absence of employe complaints is a positive sign. Employes may be expressing themselves through other channels: meetings with fellow employes, union representatives, government agents; or through passive-aggressive behavior such as work slowdowns, carelessness, tardiness, absenteeism, and apathy. These can be symptoms that employes feel other means of participation are unavailable to them. If Myth Five undergirds your organization's communications program, be prepared for some unpleasant surprises.

So much for the worst case. Consider now a situation in the best-case category.

Suppose your organization's senior official writes a letter directing that all employes are to do—or refrain from doing—a certain thing. Suppose further that the letter is well-written and well-founded and that the executive's intentions are clearly in the best interests of the organization. On the surface there may seem little reason why communication with employes should not occur and the directive not be followed.

Now, let's go deeper.

The letter is addressed "to all employes." It may or may not reach *all* employes for a variety of reasons, including absences, faulty addressing, mistakes in the mailroom.

On the other hand, it may be delivered through management channels, in which case its destiny rides with the supervisors —or more likely, with their secretaries. Again, difficulties encountered in delivery may determine the number of employes who actually receive the letter. And this is only the first hurdle to be surmounted before communication can be achieved.

Let's assume now that all employes do in fact receive the letter. Will they all respond in the manner the executive intends? Will they all obey the directive? Of course not. Certain employes will misunderstand either the message or its applicability to them. Others will get the message, yet ignore it.

Some employes will disregard the directive because of an almost childlike notion that it's fun to try to beat the system, that regulations are for everyone else. Others may believe that the directive is ridiculous and ought to be ignored. Still other employes, fortunately relatively few, will take the position that no high muck-a-muck is going to tell them what to do.

Most employes will follow the directive, though with varying degrees of enthusiasm and fidelity. However, despite this more or less acceptable behavior, the executive's directive is not followed precisely. Problems occur when the executive is not sufficiently savvy to know in advance that this will be the case.

Suppose, now, that the executive chooses a different route. Let's say he addresses his letter to "all supervisors" rather than to "all employes," and that he directs the management people to pass the message to their employes. Will they? Same answer: No.

Similar problems in delivery will occur. Furthermore, management group attitudes and responses will resemble those of employes generally. But there will be a new twist too—an "English" applied by the management people.

In the first instance, numerous employes amended and interpreted the document's meaning to suit themselves. Here the management people toy with the message, each de-emphasizing what he views as unimportant, embellishing what he regards as most important. Conclusion: Everyone, regardless of his position, level of loyalty to the organization, and commitment to doing a good job, works with a certain amount of self-interest.

This inherently human phenomenon can be an asset or an obstacle to organizational performance, depending on how well it's understood, and whether it's channeled or ignored by management people.

Individual self-interest, which, paradoxically, we're inclined to see as motivational in ourselves and disruptive in others, outweighs all other factors associated with receptiveness and responsiveness to messages. As regards the executive's directive, those people who want to comply because they feel such a response is in their best interest (for either positive or negative reasons) usually will, even when they disagree with the directive. Those who want to resist in some way usually will, in forms both subtle and overt.

The executive's letter can only initiate communication. It's not the end-product, as is so often assumed. The directive contained in the letter amounts to a new element injected into an existing environment—the communication climate. Employe receptiveness and responsiveness to the directive will be determined more by the climate—i.e., employe perception of the relationship between themselves and the organization, and of what response is in their individual best interest—than by the words and medium used to convey the directive. The reason: People communicate. Things do not.

Myth No. 6

Skill in communication comes from God. It's the birthright of certain people who, when they grow up, specialize in something called communications. Organizations employ such people and assign them occupational titles, like communicator. Everyone else is inadequate in the role.

Here's perhaps the greatest rip-off of all. But the myth presumably had to arise in an age of specialization. There are lots of reasons for this, the most obvious being that a complex society makes for complicated problems in understanding the nature of your various audiences. Specialists can help, and often must perform certain tasks. But the specialists can do you in. They can make you rely on them too heavily. This applies to all professions. Everyone guards his own rice bowl.

Then there's you and the others who comprise the client roster for professional communicators. When you're unwilling to face the realities of employe/management communication (see especially Chapters Two and Three), when you're too lazy to take the time and do the work required to form positive relation-

ships (you call it being too busy), when you're satisfied with your level of ineptitude—you send for us. And you expect us to arrive like Messianic messengers, bearing solutions for all your problems. We may be able to temporarily alleviate some problems, but there's no way we can relieve you of your responsibility. Even for money.

That's a heavy message, deliberately delivered with a hammer. Why? Mostly because it's well known that in all activities involving success and failure, *attitude* is the key determinant of outcome. Winners and losers tend to think like what they are. Now consider:

- Inasmuch as modern mythology makes communication a practice for specialists, rather than a role for everyone, the subject has become shrouded in mystery, much like the practice of brain surgery. Consequently the specialists are rewarded and the laymen's inadequacies are reinforced.

- Since organizations employ professional communicators, other employes feel relieved of any responsibility for communication. After all, the unspoken illogic goes, if we have professional communicators on the payroll, you must have to be a professional communicator in order to communicate well. And since I'm not a professional communicator, and therefore can't communicate well, why should I communicate at all? To do so might prove embarrassing because I can't possibly be adequate in the role of communicator.
- There's a self-fulfilling prophecy in action. We predict failure, then follow a course which assures its occurrence. Absurd? Certainly. Not because this doesn't happen, but because it *does*. And with great frequency. This view has acquired tacit, wide-spread acceptance as organizations have grown, further dividing the divisions of labor by constantly adding new components to perform increasingly specialized work.
- In the process, parochialism has achieved added destructive potential. It's now more or less accepted that being an engineer, for instance, isn't the same as being a communicator. How could it be? Engineers are on the second floor, communicators on the third.
- Just as specialization may breed parochialism, it can also arouse confusion. Our efforts, intentional or accidental, to isolate communication from other aspects of living, working, and our very *being* seriously impede our ability to do the one thing we're born to do: communicate.

Here is a supervisor. See him "managing" people. In this picture, we see him performing his "human relations" role. Here he's engaged in "problem solving." In the next shot he is "planning," and here we see him "reporting" on the day's activities. And in the final frame, he's "communicating."

If we don't soon learn and act as if we believe and understand that management, human relations, and psychology, indeed the performance of all functions involving human beings and their interactions—and communication—are all approximately the same thing, you can color the future dismal for us and our institutions.

It's true that most people are inept as communicators. Few develop the sensitivity and listening ability essential to the two-way process which results in communication. In fact, a lot of so-called professionals lack these qualities too. However, for you this need not be a permanent condition, mythology notwithstanding. Indeed, it mustn't be if you are to fulfill your responsibilities as a supervisor.

Consider your role as compared to that of the professional communicators on your organizations' payroll—either as full-time employes or as consultants. The professionals may do your firm's advertising and public relations. Perhaps they produce the employe newspaper or other house organ, maintain the bulletin boards, write executive speeches, prepare management audiovisual presentations, even operate a closed-circuit TV network within your facility.

While such formal communications programs are valuable and can enhance operating efficiency, they are less essential to an organization's health and welfare than the informal program. And that's where the supervisors come in.

The professionals may generate excellent one-way communication programs, but they don't participate daily with line employes in the two-way process. That's the supervisor's role. And it's the supervisors who must create the climate for positive relationships and thus communication. These are two reasons why supervisors represent the first-line of defense for an organization's best interests:

1. Supervisors create the climate because it is they who manage the people who produce the organization's product.
2. While professional communicators can and should work with the supervisors, they can't spend all their time in the shops and offices monitoring communication practices. And they can not—and must not—interpose themselves between the supervisors and their employes. Not unless dissension is an organizational goal.

Specialists and senior managers can help make a good climate better, but they can't make a bad one good except through the supervisors. They can, however, make a good climate bad by undermining the supervisors.

Supervisors represent the basic strength (or weakness) of their organizations. No matter how capable as individuals or as a group the top management or the communications specialists may be, if the supervisors are incompetent or improperly equipped as people-managers—as communicators—the entire organization is weak, less productive and profitable than it could be.

The problems you encounter every day: employe errors caused by carelessness, lack of motivation, information or training; difficulties in meeting schedules or cost budgets; problems stemming from insufficient upper-management direction—all result from and in human failure. And all are communication problems.

When we consistently behave as if there's a uniqueness about communication, making it something separate from the rest of living, we expand the gap between problems and solutions. We virtually preclude an understanding of our problems when we fail to perceive their relationship to faulty communication.

Performance goals are achieved by people. People function together through communication. When communication fails, organizations function poorly—and sometimes they cease to function at all.

Until we regard communication as a function which is crucial to both individual and collective accomplishment we'll make little genuine progress toward improved human relationships and more cooperative, efficient employe interfaces. Until then, these myths, like the preceding mysteries, will persist because we'll allow them to.

People—all of us—are responsible for the mysteries and myths which pervade our organizations. We create them or allow them to be created and perpetrated. Through our passive acceptance, we permit them to go unexplored, unchallenged, unchecked.

But the mysteries can be solved, the myths exploded, if only more of us will rely on the potency of the question mark and summon the courage to ask: "Why?"

Supervisors who want to remedy these situations, who desire more flexibility in managing their functions—which means more freedom for themselves and their employes—must do at least two things. First, examine and analyze personal and organizational attitudes. Determine who seems to obstruct communication. Is it them? Or me? Second, be prepared to work patiently toward altering these attitudes and clearing a new path for future improvement.

It's you, not top management, who must prove your capability and commitment to constructive change. And here, balance is essential. If you approach the challenge lackadaisically, as if everything will change in time anyhow, you'll fail. If you approach it hostilely, as if previously you've been denied some Constitutional right, you'll fail—maybe even get fired. If you approach it with an excess of overt diligence, you'll be viewed as a threat by one or more top managers, and, again, you'll fail. It's tricky business.

However, if you begin with your group, your boss, your peers, you can gradually bring about the changes in human resource management you desire. But it must be done professionally and with patience.

Take a lesson from the duck. As someone once said: The duck is an admirable creature—serene on the pond's surface and paddling like hell underneath.

Admirable. And he always seems to get where he's going.

Chapter 9

All God's Children Got Models

In early childhood, before we're capable of manipulating verbal symbols—words—much of our learning derives from models: people whose behavior we imitate. But it doesn't stop there.

As adults, our personal and professional development are still influenced by models. However, experience and intellectual growth expand our spectrum of model-candidates and liberate us from the bondage of indiscriminate imitation. We acquire selectivity. We learn to screen potential models; emulate some, reject others. We can choose.

But we don't always exercise the option. Sometimes, like children, we fail to differentiate. Occasionally we may more or less slip into a model mold without knowing why. We're even prone to adopt model styles without being aware that we've done so. This lack of awareness can cause us to believe that our models imitate or otherwise agree with our behavior rather than the other way around. Such failures in awareness and objectivity transport us on some of our biggest ego-trips.

We Too Are Models

We're all influenced by models. But more importantly here, we're all potential models for other people. Those who occupy any position of authority must deal consciously and continually with this reality and behave accordingly. The communication climate depends on it.

Just as a person may unconsciously follow the example of another, the model himself is usually unaware of his role. By implication, this imposes a hefty responsibility on supervisors. Their behavior generally sets a pattern for relationships throughout the entire organization.

Employes constantly observe, evaluate, and discuss management conduct. Not for fun; for profit. From such assessments they develop opinions and attitudes regarding the firm as a place to live one's work life.

Every supervisor, no matter which rung of the organization ladder he stands on, represents a success symbol to his employes. This has nothing whatever to do with whether the supervisor is admired or despised; whether his behavior is respected or deplored. To his employes, the supervisor has "made it" in the organization. Consequently, his behavior, they believe, shows a way to (pick one): survive, get along, get ahead.

There's yet another aspect of the modeling phenomenon that should be considered. This has to do with the interactions—the relationships—of the management people themselves. Employes observe these too, noting, for instance, cooperativeness and courtesy on the positive side, jealousies and pettiness on the negative. What emerges from their evaluation amounts to an unwritten standard of conduct—which all organizations have—and this standard is more forceful than any published procedure. The sum of these factors produces what may be referred to as the work environment. But you can also call it the communication climate because they are precisely the same thing.

Even at a Distance

Consider also that it's unnecessary that people have direct, personal contact with those who emerge as their models. Certain of our models may be people we know intimately, others we may know only casually. Still others, however, we may never meet; our only contact with them will be symbolic. But no matter: symbolism pervades all model relationships.

The general reputation of a senior manager in your organization, coupled with some second-hand information from a credible source regarding the executive's business acumen and management practices, may influence your own management style. If so, the executive becomes a model for you. Your contact with him is solely symbolic. Your information is perhaps unverifiable. Nevertheless, you may select this model because emulation of the executive seems to mark a route to success in your organization or because his performance, as you perceive it, coincides with and thus reinforces your own notions on the practice of management.

However, in such cases, your observations are superficial. They indicate what the person-model *seems* to be about, what he appears to represent; yet these are factors on which we frequently base our choices of models. In the absence of familiarity or at least some personal contact with the model, our perceptive powers operate at long range, and our imagination plays a prominent part in the selection process. Obviously, risky business.

What Do You Want?

Whether we select a model instinctively or consciously we do so because something about another person strikes us as worthy of emulation. The reasons underlying our choices vary with our individual personalities and circumstances; yet for all of us the process seems to fulfill some psychological need—real or imagined, vital or trivial. Fortunately, there are model-candidates available to suit every personality, illustrate every character trait, assist in the achievement of every goal. Identifying appropriate models should not be difficult once you identify your own goals, understand your own personality, and develop at least the rudiments of a management philosophy. But of course there's the rub . . . the Catch 22, as it were.

In truth, most of us don't really know what we want out of life beyond the next raise or promotion. Many of us are uncertain of what we're willing to put into life in order to achieve those rewards we can identify. As for a management philosophy, don't we tend to be concrete on what we expect of others, yet fairly fuzzy regarding standards of performance for ourselves?

Small wonder, then, that we so often slip and slide into management patterns we acquire from other managers, especially those who are senior to us in either status or experience. Unfortunately, most of them are slipping and sliding too; operating without specific personal goals and a clear philosophy. So why not be different? Reverse the process. Think about your philosophy and itemize your goals first, then select your management models.

This approach you'll find more practical and productive. Using it, you'll have the added satisfaction of knowing who you are, what you want to be, and how much energy and other precious personal resources you're willing and able to expend on behalf of your organization and your career.

It's your choice, your career. So why allow circumstance and happenstance to determine your course? Hopefully, the following chapters will help.

Chapter 10

Playing to Win

Positive Attitude

"Playing to Win" is a familiar term to sports enthusiasts. It suggests that playing to win isn't the same as merely playing a game. Which it definitely is not. And there's hardly a competitive sports buff who doesn't realize instantly what a broadcaster means when he says that a team or individual "really came to play!"

In athletics, in business, in every aspect of life, certain characteristics separate the true professionals from everybody else. Ability, training, experience, and a few breaks are all important factors on the field or on the job. However, nothing influences success more than that quality we call a *positive attitude.*

The importance of attitude varies little between endeavors or occupations, or between super-star and supervisor. Under the umbrella of positive attitude are such characteristics as a driving desire for excellence in one's field or occupation; the courage to innovate, the daring to be different; the determination to hang-in there when confronted with adversity and setbacks. These are among the traits we often see in people we regard as successful.

Success, like communication, almost defies definition. It, too, means different things to different people. Definitions of success are necessarily subjective and require an individual value judgment. Some people, however, use this value judgment as a crutch for underachievement. Constructed from the old cliché that what you are is more important than what you become, there's an implication that in order to achieve success you must often sublimate your feelings for humanity and become less good as a person. Color this attitude cop-out.

Each person must ask himself: "What reward do I want for my life's work? Money? Prestige? Other recognition? Security? What? When, if ever, can I say, 'I'm content. . . I've made it.'?" Each person judges for himself what the reward should be and how much is enough.

Success may be stimulated by professional pride—the feeling that comes from excelling at your job and knowing that you do. The question is: "Is that enough? Is it enough for me to know that I excel? Or do I want other people to know it too?" Many people who think about it at all probably would like to be accepted for their ability. This acceptance constitutes a form of reward. But consider also that acceptance, respect and superstar status are on the same continuum. A person's ambition frequently determines the point on which his version of reward sufficiency lies.

Obviously your landing in the Hall of Fame or on Executive Row depends on more factors than your personal desire or ambition to do so. Consider these three characteristics of successful people:

1. They usually make a conscious decision to be successful. This becomes an objective. There are exceptions, of course, but people don't usually stumble into success. There simply are not that many boss's daughters to go around.
2. They establish goals which they periodically adjust in order to capitalize on new opportunities, circumvent career constraints as they arise, or to conform to reality as they learn more about their ability.

3. They never lose sight of their objective—success as they define it—nor do they permit temporary setbacks to diminish the vigor with which they pursue that objective. Collaterally, they often utilize numerous seemingly small achievements as the building blocks for the attainment of the ultimate objective.

We can reduce each of these thoughts to a single word descriptive of the traits involved: decisiveness; flexibility; perseverance.

Attitude as a Success Factor

The subject of each of the preceding statements is not success as a communicator, or as a supervisor, or as any other specific thing, for that matter. Establishing the desire to be successful in a given field and setting the goals necessary to achieve that success is secondary here to developing the attitude that makes accomplishment possible. *Attitude* constitutes the subject of each statement, and a positive attitude is, itself, a form of success.

The alternative to success is not failure. To try but not succeed—in anything—is to fail, but only by accepting your defeat as a way of life can you fail as a person.

Many people fail *themselves* because they shy away from life's challenges. They refuse to take the risks or make the decisions that could result in defeat—or success.

Is there a more "negative" attitude than that of the defeatist—the person who denies himself the most glorious aspect of his being: the freedom to choose? Tragically, many people chain themselves to a single decision—that they will avoid risks. This, of course, assures that they will never be chastized for failures. How can they fail? They never really chanced anything.

Choices, options, alternatives surround us. And if we live in a society and work in organizations that are in any way worthwhile we are entitled to at least three freedoms:

- The freedom to succeed,
- The freedom to fail,
- The freedom to try again.

Even if we make a bad decision, we're still free to make a new one. Even should we fail, we can still pick up our ego-marbles and start over. Successful people don't shrink from decisions, they welcome them as opportunities.

Flexibility (the opposite of rigidity) enables people to adjust to meet changing situations. You must be flexible in order to evaluate opportunities, shift goals, or negotiate with other people. Flexibility equates with what's often called an "open mind."

Refer again to the three characteristics of successful people. Notice that the second statement says that successful people establish goals—not *a* goal. That's important. There are intermediate steps along the path leading to the objective. They operate as a hedge against frustration. Arriving at your objective may take considerable time. Along the way, it's helpful to have a series of goals—call them stepping stones or milestones—the achievement of which will bring you at least temporary satisfaction. For example, if your objective is to be making a certain amount of money before you retire—say $500 a week—and today you make $250 a week, you might set a goal to make $275 by a certain year, $300 by another date, and so forth. That way, you're always achieving, always moving.

Your goal may be stated as a specific job or as a certain level of professional proficiency or organizational stature. If your goal is a specific job—your boss's, for instance—your milestone might therefore be to become his assistant. Or if that doesn't seem practical you might look elsewhere and take a job as someone else's assistant, but with the idea of acquiring the training and experience to one day assume a job similar to your boss's. Maybe even his when he moves on.

Should you aspire to a top management post the course is much the same. However, you'll need a broader plan—one with many

more options—an elastic attitude, lots of luck, plenty of patience, and the ability and determination to persevere through a series of partial successes and outright setbacks.

Setbacks Aren't Always Drawbacks

Be prepared for the setbacks. At one time or another you may be passed over for a promotion. You may not always get raises when you think you deserve them. Others will get jobs or recognition which you believe rightfully belong to you. These situations, and others, actually are opportunities—sometimes well disguised, but opportunities nonetheless. Rather than providing you with an excuse for abandoning your objective, setbacks provide a backdrop against which you can evaluate yourself, your objective and goals, and your chances for achieving them. The following questions illustrate the kind of check list you might want to use:

- In the light of current circumstances, is the objective beyond my capability?
- Is it time to set a new objective? New goals?
- Is it time to seek a different opportunity elsewhere?
- Is my current organization or group stifling rather than stimulating my initiative?
- What does this setback tell me about management's regard for my ability and for the value of my contribution?
- How does this rating jibe with my own evaluation of my ability and worth to the organization?
- Are my strengths really what I thought they were?
- Am I as strong in them as I thought I was?
- Have I properly evaluated my weaknesses?
- Have I done all I can to overcome my weaknesses?
- Is this really a setback, or do I feel that it is merely because I'm anxious to move ahead?
- Have I given myself sufficient time to achieve this goal?

Self-evaluation isn't easy but it is necessary. It's difficult to appraise yourself, since complete objectivity is impossible. Once you set a goal, you'll become emotionally involved in its attainment. Furthermore, there are many things about yourself that you really don't know. Your initial pass at these questions should reveal a number of "I don't know's." If it doesn't, if you believe you've got all the answers (and not surprisingly the answers are all complimentary) beware. You've done a poor job of self-appraisal. This may be one reason for the setback. Think about the questions and your answers a second time.

So much for setbacks. You've got the idea now and can develop your own personalized survey—one that fits your circumstances.

Dealing with partial successes involves much the same process. If a partial success provides thrust for the attainment of your objective, it has value. If it doesn't, even if it brings more money or momentary status, it may be a detriment in disguise.

It could be a digression or even a derailment; an apparent opportunity that actually conflicts with your future best interest. Think carefully about that too.

How Hungry Are You?

You've no doubt observed that many successful people in your own organization display a voracious appetite for involvement in organizational affairs. This appetite is fueled by work, responsibility, accomplishment, and reward. It appears as an attitude toward the firm, but it usually has more to do with how such people feel about themselves.

Successful people distinguish between working and working for something. They've made two essential career decisions:

What do I want? What am I willing to *give up* to have it? And make no mistake, success is as much a giving up as it is a getting. You exchange much of your personal time and energy for the rewards of your professional life. What price are you willing to pay for this kind of success?

What has all this to do with becoming a better supervisor or a better communicator? Everything. What we've been discussing here is *intra*personal communication: Getting to know yourself, your goals, the price you'll pay to attain them.

If you're anxious to receive organizational life's rewards you must also confront its realities, anticipate and accept its risks. Everything worthwhile involves some risks. Or so it seems. No matter how well you plan or how diligently you implement your plans, sooner or later something will go wrong anyhow. You may work tirelessly and faithfully and still not succeed to the degree you desire. But you will not have failed.

Chapter 11

To Get An Even Break. . . Be Your Own Odds-Maker

Damon Runyon once said, "It may be that the race is not always to the swift or the battle to the strong, but that's the way to bet it." Sound advice for anyone preparing to wager his money, time, or energy against some future uncertainty.

Your career holds plenty of imponderables. But in the race against retirement time or in the struggle for success you can reduce some of the elements of chance. Preparation, planning, perseverance, sweat, and guts are mechanisms for converting uncertainty into possibility, possibility into probability, potential into achievement.

Avoid the Negative

Look again at Runyon's statement. In business parlance, the thought goes something like this: It may be that raises and promotions don't always go to the best qualified people, but it makes sense to work as if you believe they do.

We all know that the best qualified people don't always get promoted. Every organization has its hacks in high places; its mediocrities masquerading as managers. Knowing this is one thing. Getting hung up on it is quite another.

Rather than dwell on organizational accidents—cases where losers reap rewards while winners are ignored—concentrate on the positive side. Put your own career in perspective: What has happened? What is happening? What must happen if you are to move up the institutional ladder?

Many people fail to do this. And far too many encumber themselves with yet another attitudinal crutch. This one is constructed of platitudes like "There's no sense breaking your back around this place. You never get anywhere anyhow." And "Why knock yourself out? Promotions are a political fix. Unless you know the right people, you don't have a chance."

Unquestionably, these grumblings accurately reflect the management practices of some organizations. Many unskilled or otherwise incompetent people do succeed by virtue of their personality and personal contacts. But the critics aren't always correct.

What more natural occupation is there than that of critic. It's a job we're all born to. However, priorities pose a problem. We must decide between working to move up in an organization and trying to bring other people down. There's hardly time for both. So while you're evaluating the management practices of your organization, be sure to evaluate the personality and contribution of the critics you encounter there. It's not uncommon to discover that those who complain the most contribute the least.

Some people constantly engage in an institutionalized version of the kids' game, "King of the Mountain"—only here the contributors hold the crest while the complainers scramble to put them down.

A Check List

Even in the best managed organizations, you'll find errors in judgment. There's always some individual incompetence and, most likely, a bit of nepotism. Perhaps a few—or even many—key contributors will be disgruntled with one or more aspects of their job or firm. But certain people have little time for anything but complaining. You'll do well to avoid such people. Go a step further. Ask yourself some questions about the organization and about its people. Try these for a start:

- Does this organization offer genuine promotional opportunities? Is there a promotion system, or is it a "buddy" system?
- Do the Personnel people screen and recommend candidates for promotion, or do managers rely on "hallway recruiting?"
- When promotions come up, what personal and professional characteristics appear to make the greatest impression on management?
- Are hard work, dedication, loyalty, and ability to get things done the primary promotional considerations? If not, what standard does management use?
- What common qualities did the last three people who were promoted have?
- What is my boss's stated policy on promotions? Do his words jibe with his actions? Do I trust him?
- If the decision were mine, would I promote any of the people who complain the most about the system? Looking at it another way, how good are they at their jobs?
- If the decision were mine, would I promote me?
- Of the most vocally dissatisfied, how long have I known them? How long have they been here? How long have they been critical of the organization? Why are they still here?
- Who are these "buddies" of management who got the "political" promotions? Personal relationships notwithstanding, did they deserve the promotions?
- Given the choice, would I have promoted any of them?
- If not, why not?
- What's the basis of the relationships between them and their alleged "angels?" Family? Friend? Professional?
- Do I have sufficient facts to make an intelligent and valid judgment?

A check list such as this one encourages analysis, rather than reliance on hearsay or emotion. It can help you to decide between remaining with your current employer and looking elsewhere for a better opportunity. The main thing, however, is to keep your own performance, management relationships, and career aspirations firmly in mind.

Make your decisions with the same objectivity you'd utilize in selecting a new car or house. Reason is the key. Even if the so-called system seems stacked against everyone else, if it's working for you, that's an essential consideration. If it's not working for you, or if it appears that you've gone as far as you can expect to go in the organization, you've got a decision to make.

Let your career goals be your yardstick. Measure, evaluate, decide. The one thing you can't afford to do is nothing. And while you're at it, re-evaluate your goals and ambitions against your performance. How does your progress look now? Are you about where you ought to be? Behind? Ahead? If ahead, good, you got lucky. If behind, why? How can you catch up? Certainly not by just blaming someone else, or by carping about the system.

If you conclude that your organization is failing to recognize and reward you for your contribution, you're past the contemplation stage. It's time for additional action. Try conversation with your boss first. A performance review, some goal-setting, and a new personal development plan may be in order. Determine where you stand, find out where you can go.*

Once you've communicated your concern, thereby inviting more critical scrutiny of your work, you can't afford to let up. If anything, you'll have to work a little harder. It's you who has to prove something. Only you can decide how much time and effort you're willing to expend.

This sort of analysis may give you a bullet to bite. The result may clearly indicate that you should quit. It's not an easy choice, abandoning the security of a supervisory position to

---

* The boss may tell you that, too. But that's one of the risks.

seek another opportunity elsewhere. But then, nothing worthwhile seems easy.

If you are competent—and this takes another terribly objective evaluation—you probably have confidence in your own ability. Self-confidence is a yardstick against which you can measure your competence.

Besides competence and confidence, career success often requires courage—the courage to evaluate yourself and your opportunities. Fortunately, the first two usually father the third, and no three personal characteristics are more crucial to your career.

Think about it. How do you rate?

The Real World

Even if your organization routinely bestows recognition and other rewards on its supervisors whose hard work, dedication, loyalty, and effectiveness merits attention, it doesn't necessarily follow that you'll achieve your goals or your ultimate objective. You may possess all the right characteristics and credentials, you may perform ably on all assignments, yet still not attain the badges of success. This is especially true in large organizations. Why?

Many people believe that if they merely plug away and do a good job they'll eventually be rewarded. True—for those who set their goals low enough. But for those with loftier ambitions, this attitude won't do. Not in the real world.

Any manager deserving of the responsibility that goes with exercising influence on the emotional and economic destiny of others wants to reward his top performers. Selfishly, this enhances his image with superiors and peers. It also acts as a motivator for others in the work group, and encourages greater efforts from those who feel properly rewarded for their performance. Unselfishly, it just plain feels good to see an outstanding employe move ahead.

But how do you define outstanding? How do you decide who merits that rating?

You could say that *outstanding* means "doing more than is required and doing it well." This might serve as a minimum definition. However, in applying it, a manager immediately encounters a new problem. Many employes do some things well, some things exceptionally well, some things only passably well.

In other words, employes may be occasionally outstanding and sometimes mediocre. What overall rating would you give such an employe?

Satisfactory? *Good*? *Excellent*? But we're looking for *outstanding*.

Outstanding, in this context, implies consistency. How many employes, peers, or executives can you identify as consistently superior—outstanding—in their jobs? If you answer "many," management's challenge is to select the best of the best for rewards. No easy task. If you say "few," most people around here are mediocre, then there's still a problem for conscientious managers. We're dealing here with comparatives. The best of the mediocrities may seem outstanding in his current job, compared to his present group. But how does he look when we compare him to employes of the group to which a promotion would take him?

It's also possible for an outstanding performer to go virtually unnoticed. Does that seem incredible?—grounds for an indictment of management? Perhaps, in some cases. There are managers who appear to care only about getting work out and acquiring maximum recognition for themselves. But what about the "white hat" managers—the ones who want to do the best job possible—for their organization and employes, as well as themselves?

A supervisor who merely plugs away and does a good job may be buried in an organizational grave of his own making—unless someone on the surface is aware that he's plugging away and doing a good job.

No one should expect his boss to do his communication job for him. Presumably the boss has other things to do. The ultimate responsibility for your career and your progress rest on you.

Personal Public Relations

The problem for the conscientious manager is only intensified by the fact that there are so few outstanding performers. Most of us are just *average*. And the average employe and the *above average* employe blend into the same background. The question is: How do you emerge as better than average?

As you progress upward in an organization, the ranks narrow, the competition for rewards increases. It's a different league, abundantly stocked with people who know how to acquire recognition for their efforts. There are fewer rules, sharper players, higher stakes. In the world of personal P.R., senior executives are the top performers.

Consider your organization. Starting with the president and coming down through senior management ranks, you'll find people with at least three things in common. Someone or some group thinks they have ability, they're generally paid rather well, and each one during his career somehow got a message across to a number of bosses that he had the ability to handle managerial assignments, a desire for responsibility, and a concern for the organization's interests. Disregarding the organizational accidents for the moment, these executives set goals which they had the perseverance to pursue and the *chutzpah* to express.

Sound like gamesmanship? OK, if that's what you want to call it. But label it realistically. It's the success game in corporate America. Make your own value judgment, but if you decide to play, know the rules.. They indicate how the people who get ahead get ahead.

The President of the United States or the president of a corporation didn't attain his position by concealing his abilities or ambitions. Such people don't wait for discovery. They usually initiate the event. They're not always blatant, but they are aggressive.

Each in their own way, successful people evaluate themselves—their assets and liabilities; set goals which compliment their strong suits and circumvent their shortcomings; work to overcome present and potential liabilities; and communicate, in some way, their accomplishments.

You have only one product to sell: yourself. And successful people do this successfully. It may be that "the meek shall inherit the earth"—but the timid do not inherit the corporations. You needn't be obnoxious or cruel or deceitful to be aggressive, but you must be ambitious.

Personal public relations should aim at honestly communicating your achievements and attributes. It relies on doing the job first, getting the credit later. Strive for both, but in that order. Your credibility depends on it.

What kind of person says, in effect, "I can run this organization better than anyone else. I should be the company president"? Is he really any different from others?

In many ways, no—except in his attitude. He feels he's got something to say, something to offer. He believes, really believes, that he's the best qualified person for the job. Call it conceit, call it courage; but whatever it is, it's the attitude that keeps corporate America and its organizations going, for better or worse. You decide, but make it a real-world decision.

Getting Ahead. . . And Keeping it

Obviously, not everyone can attain the top offices. We all have limitations imposed by our intellect, emotional development, and talent. But we can get the most from what we've got, and we can substitute skills we have in abundance for those in which we're deficient. Hard work is a great equalizer—as is a sturdy self-concept.

What some people have in talent, or so-called natural ability, other people have in dogged determination. Maybe there's such a thing as having a talent for hard work.

Look around your organization. You'll find many superiors who don't have as much talent as you do. Many may not be as bright as you. Perhaps many aren't as proficient as supervisors. How did they get their jobs? You're often asked that question, you say? But have you really thought about a possible answer?

Remember that in any given situation most of us are just average—whatever that means. However, some people excel by virtue of their aspirations and their willingness to do the work required to attain them. That trait is anything but average. There's an old Greek proverb: Before the altar of success the high gods have placed sweat.

We've all got some talent (natural ability), some skill (acquired ability), something special to offer—the latter provided we believe we do and take the time, make the effort to determine what it is. It may be nothing great, but it's probably something useful. Uncovering and utilizing that something can become its own reward. Call it satisfaction—the satisfaction of maximizing our ability, achieving our potential. It's a contribution to self and thus to self-concept.

Many of us claim we have much to offer an organization without really believing it. Not believing in ourselves, we lack faith in others. When words substitute for actions, work is avoided, failure assured. And meaningless work must be among the toughest failures to take. Why adopt such a model? There's a better way, a more rewarding role.

The ambitious supervisor keeps his management informed of his activities as a matter of course. Sometimes, it's a requirement that he report on a periodic basis. How well he does that job, and how effectively he demonstrates his worth to his superiors, depends as much on the supervisor's goals and attitudes toward the boss, the organization, and the nature of his achievements as it does on his skills. Maybe more so. If he feels his job is meaningless, it's likely that he'll underplay the accomplishments of his work group. But consider that every job is at least four things: the job you got and the one you make it; what it is and what it could be.

The supervisor who seeks advancement constantly looks for opportunities through which he and his work group can make an additional contribution. This way he demonstrates to management that he's thinking about the problems—and proposing solutions. Nearly everyone can enumerate an organization's problems, but few people propose realistic solutions.

Many supervisors show genuine concern for their employes and want to aid their progress where possible. A supervisor helps best when he is, himself, a respected person within the organization. The supervisor who rates high in upper management's esteem can greatly benefit his employes in good times and bad.

If management can trust a supervisor because it believes he's an interested member of the management team, even though he may be only on the first rung of the management ladder, he'll have influence. If he's just another guy who jockeys work through the shop, he'll limit not only his own horizons but those of his employes as well.

Regrettably, there is no sure system, no foolproof formula to follow in accomplishing these tasks. Your intellect, ability, and attitude toward yourself, your group, and your organization all will influence your performance, and thus your success. Your experience also will help—or hinder, depending on how you use it. But learn from experience. Don't get trapped in the cobwebs of corporate conformity.

Too often the reason we do things a certain way this year is that we did them that way last year. Too seldom does anyone ask "How effective was that procedure last year? Is it still applicable to today's circumstances? Can we improve on what we've done and learned?" Leaders dare to be different.

By developing the attitudes necessary for achievement, and by maximizing his ability and opportunities as a communicator, a supervisor can attain a high degree of credibility with management for himself and his work group.

Undeniably, *breaks*—being in the right place at the right time, having a boss who is concerned with the welfare and advancement of his employes—are vital factors in your career. Additionally, courage—the guts to modify the old ways, to blow out the cobwebs, to assume added responsibility, to volunteer for tough assignments, to put in the hours, to do the terribly hard work that's usually required to achieve your goals—is also a factor in your success equation. And if you're planning to make the run for excellence, be prepared for criticism from jealous peers, employes and even superiors who may feel threatened.

There's an expression that in every organization 10 percent of the people do 90 percent of the real work. The figures may vary between institutions, but the ratio is always lopsided. Choose your own spot on the see-saw. Do you *really* want to be a 10 percenter? If so, you'll spend a lot of time in the state of trouble. Is it worth it? You decide.

Someone once said that the world is filled with willing people —people willing to accept responsibility and people willing to let them. Each person's attitude determines the category into which he places himself.

But, again, you do have a choice. You can complacently conform and do only what's required to get by (and you probably will get by), or you can take some risks on behalf of your own career. One route is safe but boring; the other occasionally perilous but usually exciting.

Though they travel together, the shepherd is separate from the sheep. Think about it. Which are you? Make an honest self-appraisal. Pick a course. Now seems like a pretty good time to start.

Chapter 12

Your Organization—A Second Look, A New Perspective

Supervisors are paid to get other people to do work. Duties ranging from hiring and training to budgeting and reporting merely support the primary mission: managing. These activities generate work for you, but your job is to supervise the efforts of other employes. Put another way: your full-time role is that of communicator.

Knowing yourself—your nature, goals, skills, and limitations sharpens your focus on your mental and professional status. But you've still got some work to do.

Get Acquainted With Your People

You are surrounded by people whose support you need. Irrespective of your aspirations, be they lofty or modest, it's doubtful that you'll achieve them alone. Organization and hermitage are not synonyms.

Other people influence your career, your performance, your disposition and behavior. Obviously these people constitute an important audience for you. Two questions: Who are they? How well do you know them?

As a minimum, *they* are your boss, your peers, and your employes. *They* are the people with whom you work most frequently and directly. You know that, of course, but how well do you know the people involved? Do you have sufficient information on each member of this audience to know who you can rely on in a crisis, who you can trust with sensitive information? Which employes require the most supervision and which the least? Who among your fellow supervisors is a cheap-shot artist? Will your boss defend you if you make an innovative move that fails? Under what circumstances won't he support you?

Nor does it hurt to know some personal things about people in this audience. Not bra sizes or who wears striped shorts. Rather, conversational items—things that indicate your interest in your associates as individuals. Who just got a promotion? Whose wife had a baby? Whose husband is ill? Who has what hobby? Who likes sports, art, music?

As individuals, what are their predominant personality traits? Where do they live? Where were they born? Where did they go to school? What are their attitudes toward work generally? This job? This organization? What aspirations and ambitions do they have?

Every person is a product of his experience. Do you know enough about those people in your primary audience to understand at least some of the reasons behind their attitudes, interests, behavior?

There are other questions, other factors which you can easily identify and catalog. Perhaps you already know a great deal about your associates. You may even know more than you think you do. But a good and helpful exercise is to write down what you know. Exercise your recall ability.

Don't regard this as a gimmick or game. It's neither. It's mental conditioning. The exercise does for you what preseason training does for athletes: gets you ready—in your case, ready to communicate. There's no suggestion here that you become a probing, prying gossip broker, spending your day digging into the details of people's private lives. Quite the contrary. A gossip's concern is only for himself and his supposed status as bearer of big news. A successful supervisor shows that he gives

a damn about people other than himself. He has a visible interest in his associates as people.

Do the exercise once and you won't have to repeat it. Nor will it be necessary to keep your notes. One time through and your mind will thenceforth maintain the catalog. And you won't have to ask many questions on the personal stuff either. Just record what people tell you—and probably have been telling you all along. Only now, pay attention, if you haven't done so in the past.

When people sense that you're interested in them, that their concerns are at least momentarily important to you, they'll gladly share them with you—and be grateful for the opportunity. So what's the bottom line? What do you gain from all this? Try these rewards:

- Perspective: a greater knowledge of the people who surround you. It provides a better view of how they can help you and where you may be able to assist them.
- Humility: a prerequisite for most success, but especially for contentment. Showing interest in others and listening to their interests and concerns takes your ego-eye off yourself, if only briefly. But even a little is a lot for some of us.
- Credibility: an essential for supervisors. If you're perceived to be genuine as a human being, you'll be believable as a boss.
- Security: an inner confidence, which is also a reward. You'll know who you can entrust with what assignments, how daring you can afford to be in your management practices, and the consequences of a myriad possible decisions involving your associates but affecting your life.
- Cooperation: the place where we began. To get it you must give it. But you must know who requires your help, how much and when? Also, who won't cooperate with you? Why? What are some strategies for turning those folks around? Generally, however, people will support you willingly, albeit within the constraints imposed by their ability and schedules, provided your track record as an interested, humanistic supervisor makes you a good bet.

When people on whom you must rely believe they can count on you, you've got *quid pro quo*, a selfish but nonetheless sound basis for a working relationship. By comparing the information acquired here with your self-evaluation model, you may conclude that for personal and/or professional reasons a different set of associates would be desirable—your respective interests, attitudes, and ambitions being dramatically disparate. If such a change is necessary, make it. But make the model first.

You Gotta Know The Territory

Organizations develop personalities, as your own experience probably confirms. They are, after all, collections of people, and like individuals they strive for identity. Along the way, each one acquires characteristics and combinations of traits which make it qualitatively different from other organizations.

As with individuals occupied in common endeavors, organizations may share characteristics with others engaged in similar enterprises. In fact, an organization's personality often indicates the nature of its business. However, each one usually is somewhat unique in its response to environmental influences, such as those exerted by customers, competitors, and cognizant government agencies. Put another way: Each organization reacts in its own way to pressure and to politics.

Each organization has its own political system, its in-house political games. Furthermore, even more so than for individuals, an organization's personality is a product of traditions. The organization in which you're employed, unless it's a very young one, reflects not only the personalities of its current managers but also those of preceding generations of managers. Its personality is stamped with all the successes and failures that evoked changes in policies and practices.

Individual behavior is a function of genetic plus environmental effects. The result is personality. An individual's experiences alter his behavior, change aspects of his personality. Maturation and other development factors cause individuals to eliminate some traits and acquire new ones. The old is, in a sense, discarded. Not so with organizations.

A new policy or operational method usually issues directly from the old. The former way is refurbished, not abandoned; it's the point of departure for the new approach. And organizations don't easily discard their traditions. Sometimes, the marriage defies dissolution.

Organizations acquire personality through accumulation—the cumulative influence of the management group personalities responsible for its operations. In long-established corporations, today's managers are part of a chain that has strong links with the past. New policies, practices, and procedures are commonly superimposed over the old. What results is a buildup effect analogous to what occurs if you repeatedly add new coats of paint to a surface without removing the old paint.

An organization's personality reveals itself most through policies, operating procedures and management practices. Although these are determined mostly by top management, they don't always reflect the personal preferences or personalities of the individuals involved.

Senior staff and committee decisions are often the result of compromise. In many instances, the group's judgment will resemble a decision which its members might have made independently. However, decisions always bear the mark of the group and, more importantly, reveal the personality of the organization. Therefore, it's essential that you identify your organization's personality characteristics and evaluate the processes through which this personality manifests itself.

A Guide To Organization Personality

- Do you know your organization's history?
- How much do you know about your firm's founders and their traits?
- Do you have an Employe Relations component? If so, do other managers support it or fight it?
- Do you have an employe handbook? A management practices guide?
- Do you know the product line?
- Are people proud to work for your organization?
- Are managers proud to be managers? Do they enjoy the role?
- Do employes have confidence in top management? At what level, if any, does confidence break down?
- How "deep" is management? Are there good "backups" for the senior executives?

- Do employes have genuine advancement opportunities?
- Does management willingly change policies, procedures, and practices as circumstances warrant, or does change require crisis?
- Do policies, procedures, and practices make sense? Do they make work easier or more difficult?
- Are traditions touchstones or millstones? Is experience a guidepost or hitching post?
- Is management authoritarian? Realistic? Concerned?
- What are the predominant traits of your senior managers?
- How does your organization's management compare with that (those) of your friends and associates in other organizations?
- Is employe treatment equal to what's called for in policy guides?
- How are the pay and benefits compared to other organizations in your area?
- Are promotions, layoffs, and discipline handled fairly?
- Who are your major customers? Competitors?
- What influence does government have on your operations and, thus, on your management's attitudes and behavior?
- How healthy is the communication climate (employe-management relationships) in your organization, your work group?
- Are your parent organization's goals made clear to employes?
- Do employes understand the nature and operations of the business?
- Are employes told the *real* reasons for most decisions affecting them?
- Is employes' constructive contribution to the business solicited? Are employes coerced or led by management?
- Is initiative encouraged or stifled?
- Are employe suggestions investigated and, where useful, implemented? Or are they ignored?

- When employe suggestions are not implemented, are the reasons for rejection explained?
- Is there an ongoing "war of nerves" between union and management?
- Where initiative is encouraged, do people capitalize on the opportunity for the organization's benefit and their own?
- How well do employes follow instructions?
- How much faith in management do they have?
- How much does management trust employes to act responsibly?
- How much money and energy are lost because of poor guidance, lack of employe initiative, unclear instructions?
- How often is useless work performed because supervisors misunderstand assignments or instructions from upper management?
- With what frequency must you perform whimsical assignments because your boss or others are trying to impress superiors?
- Do you have free-flowing communication with your boss or does he treat you like an order-taker?

Answers to questions such as these aid in assessing your organization's personality, and thus the climate in which you work. People influence the organization—and they have the power to change it. But it also happens that the organizational entity—as if it were human—influences the behavior and personalities of the people who inhabit it.*

* The point here comes from my own experience at GE. For instance, you can hear expressions such as "That's not the way GE does things." This is roughly equivalent to the military admonition regarding conduct unbecoming an officer and gentleman. As used by some managers I've known, such statements implied that certain activities were simply inappropriate or undignified, and therefore not the GE way. To them, being a GE manager is a very special responsibility and a genuine reward. Their attitudes are personal, yet these attitudes have one hell of a lot to do with GE's personality. Certain traditions are still respected, and I think that's beautiful.

Whatever career course you select, whichever employer you choose, your path will be smoother, your decisions sounder, once you've analyzed your own personality and compared your aspirations and management style to the personality characteristics of your current or prospective organization.

One final thought: You can also build a model of your ideal organization—the one you'd regard as having the most favorable communication and career climate. Then compare that to your current environment. You may not enjoy the results, but at least you'll understand the difference between what you have and what you're searching for.

People Models—Help Or Hindrance?

As noted earlier, we usually select people-models casually, even unconsciously. Consequently, our model choices are often poor ones that do little to further our management mission or aid in attainment of career goals. Obviously there are no perfect people—those whose example will assist us in every aspect of our own lives—but we can make selective and intelligent choices.

Supervisors, like others, continue to be influenced by models. These may be helpful to you in either a positive or negative sense. Your own manager, for instance, may display personal and management characteristics which you either accept as the way you want to go or reject as incompatible with your personality and views. Be careful to retain this independent perspective, otherwise you may adopt an inappropriate model style. It's a poor marriage. Once separated from that person-model, you'll have no style, no philosophy, no pattern of your own to rely on. You could be left mired in uncertainty while issues requiring action and attention surround you.

Regard emulation of any person-model as a training exercise only. Don't get fixated. Models can help get you started in a new job or performance area. New and different models are beneficial as new situations confront you. But be your own person. Learn. Extend. Grow.

You must evaluate a model's behavior as you do your own—i.e., as objectively as possible. Regardless of your fondness for a person, and no matter how successful he may seem, if his management style is rigid and authoritarian, abandon him as a management model. It may be that his technical ability is such that top management is willing to overlook his supervisory behavior. Perhaps his technical skill is required at the supervisory level and no suitable replacement has yet been found. In any case, you've got a bad management model. Look for another.

Your search for appropriate models should lead you to more than one person. This procedure is not unlike that of a novelist who builds models which in stories we call characters. The physical and personality traits of these story-people may be drawn from the real-life characteristics of many people: The face of one, the body of another, one person's laugh, another's temper, and so on.

A management style may be constructed the same way. You need more than one model because no one is good enough at everything to serve exclusively as your model.

You may find some people whose technical skill you admire and want to emulate. Fine. But these may not be the same people you want as management models. In fact, by virtue of their personality and ability to integrate and interface with people, they may be diametrically opposite your management models. Management of people takes a different set of skills from those classified as "technical skills." The skills required to draw, fix a pipe or machine, run a press, or design a car are not the same as those needed to manage employes humanely and efficiently. Many people possess both sets of skills, but many more do not.

Keep in mind, though, that modeling is a tool. By observing, evaluating, and selectively employing the methods of various models you can accelerate your own learning process. In certain situations their successes or failures can obviate some trial-and-error effort for you. But you must understand why they succeeded or failed in a given undertaking. And it's useful to at least attempt to calculate how a failure could have been a success. This aspect of model study is potentially the most rewarding—and the most ignored. Be different.

Remember, too, that there are no duplicate people, no carbon-copy personalities alike in every detail. Methods which seemingly result in consistent success—personal or professional—for your models won't necessarily work for you. Not without modification.

Your emergence as an effective manager of people, like your

development as an individual, depends partly on your ability to capitalize on learning opportunities.

People-models offer many opportunities. But the ability to differentiate between appropriate model methods and styles and those unsuited to your own philosophy, goals, and pull of personality is vital. You develop that by finding out about yourself first.

Chapter 13

The Mix-and-Match Model

Do you frequently feel run down? Frustrated with your job? Uncomfortable with your associates? Disillusioned with your organization? Discouraged by your career progress? Disappointed with your life's course? If so the reason might not be tired blood.

You may be in the wrong job. Perhaps you're surrounded by people with whom you share few interests. Or maybe you're traveling an incorrect career route, using ill-defined goals as your road map and an inappropriate organization as your vehicle. Here's one kind of bad trip anyone can take.

Some Get Trapped

Corporate America is a veritable labor camp for the unwary and the unlucky. Some inhabitants are confined by unfortunate circumstances. Others, however, have imprisoned themselves in an unsuitable occupation, profession, career, or company. This applies to employes, to supervisors, and even to senior executives. For some, escape seems improbable; for others, impossible. Age, seniority, pension credits, status, and income level guard the camp. Misery shares each cell.

This problem affects interpersonal communication practices involving managers and employes because it affects people's self-concepts, and thus their attitudes.

Our concern here is with you and your fellow management people. The badges of office—authority, bigger salary, better office, and the like—give the appearance of success. However, for many managers, they represent reminders of their failure to find psychically satisfying work before economic and social factors took them prisoner. Some fail at goal-setting, but many of us simply lack the courage to pursue our dreams. Routinely, the resulting frustration, guilt, or fear of the financial consequences that a change in life style might bring conspires with discontent to, in a sense, immobilize the person so afflicted. He's precluded from selecting a new life course, but he's dissatisfied with the one he's on. He's hung-up in the middle. It's unlikely that superiors who feel trapped themselves will be free and open with their employes.

We're talking about real people with genuine problems. They're in your organization. They're in all organizations. And they occupy positions at every echelon, every social stratum.

The disenchantment or discontent often issues from an intrapersonal communication breakdown, but it always interferes with interpersonal relationships. Self-respect necessarily precedes respect for others.

Fear is only occasionally a gun at your head. More often, it's a gun *in* your head. We all have one, but for some of us it's got a hair-trigger. Those are special cases. Most of us, however, can keep the weapon disarmed by getting to know ourselves, dealing with what we uncover, improving where we can—and most of all, learning to like ourselves as best we're able.

Introspection Can Be Enlightening

This is the dialogue approach. Have a conversation with yourself. Find a place that's confortable and relaxing for you. Getting away from your normal work or home environment may be helpful. Try a walk on the beach, a stroll through a park or woodland, a bicycle ride—whatever will put you in the mood for serious reflection. Let your mind drift. Observe and enjoy your surroundings to the fullest.

Once you're feeling relaxed, return to some place where you can work. This is important because you're going to work hard. Get lots of paper and something to write with. Now ask yourself three questions:

1. Who am I?
2. Where am I?
3. What do I want to be when I grow up?

You can begin by writing your name or anything else that comes into your head. But handle the questions in order and individually. Try to fill as many sheets as possible with responses to "Who am I?" before proceeding to the next question. List your personal characteristics. Use "I am" to begin each item and employ as many modifiers as necessary. For instance: "I am an independent person, but I do need the companionship and support of other people in both my personal and professional life." Consider your philosophy as a supervisor. List your personality traits. Give some thought to how other people—superiors, peers, and employes—regard you. Are you respected? Well-liked? Do others seek you out for advice, support?

Include the heavy stuff too. Be honest. If you're insecure, not as competent in your job as you should be—say so. If you dislike your profession, boss, or organization—say so. If you're fearful of losing your job or of losing yourself in your job—say so. And if you don't like yourself very much, tell yourself about it. It's a very tough assignment, but it's very rewarding work.

You'll accomplish some interesting and worthwhile things through this exercise. Probably, you've never before set down on paper your personal approach to management of people, your management philosophy. Every manager has one, it's just that few managers seem to know what it is. Now you'll know.

In the idiom of the streets: You can't tell where you're at if you don't know where you're coming from. Find out.

Once you find out, you'll be prepared to deal with the second and third questions.

"Where am I?" includes some management philosophy too. It leads to an examination of your organization—the things you like and perhaps dislike about it. It gives you a check on your financial, social, and professional progress. And it reveals something about your development as a mature or maturing supervisor. You should also be able to fill a few sheets on this subject.

"What do I want to be when I grow up?" is a facetious way of asking: "What are my goals? Where do I go from here? Where can I go? Am I on the right course? Do I want the job or profession I have now? Do I want to work for this outfit the rest of my life? If not, how much longer? What other jobs seem more appealing? Do I really like people? Is management really my bag?"

25 Thought Provokers

Your mission here is to end up with three piles of paper—one for each of the three preceding questions. The following questions should help stimulate your thought process. Each can be answered under one of the three major headings. Hopefully, you'll get the hints and expand the list, devise your own questions.

1. Do I like myself as a person? Either way, why?
2. Would I like to work for me? Why?
3. Would I like me for a friend? Why?
4. What are my five chief assets as a supervisor? As an employe of this organization?
5. Does this organization fully utilize my ability?
6. Is there sufficient challenge in my job?
7. What are my major flaws as a supervisor?
8. Who can help me overcome them?
9. What specifically don't I like about myself as a person?*
10. What have I done lately to improve?
11. Do I enjoy my job? Or is it all work? Why?

* You probably glossed over this one the first time.

12. Is this the right career field for me, my personality being what it is?
13. What field might I be as well or better suited for?
14. Where would I have to start if I made the change to that (those) field(s)? Would I lose money, status, security? How important are these things to me?
15. Do I have guts enough to change—either my flaws or my profession?
16. What job opportunities exist in the fields I think I might like? What's the going "market rate"?
17. Do I have the skills required for promotion in this organization? How far can I go?
18. Do I have the skills required to change employers or my career course? What else do I need? Am I willing to make the sacrifice? If yes, why haven't I taken action before this?
19. Is my boss a help or hindrance in my career? What can I do for him that would encourage him to do more for me?
20. Do I enjoy working with my peers and employes? Am I learning all from them that I could?
21. Is my temperament suited to management?
22. How far can I expect to go in management? Why? What impediments to promotion do I face?
23. Do other people like me? Why? What can I change? What can't I change? Do I give a damn?
24. Are the things I like and dislike about myself the same things that other people like and dislike about me? Am I an *aware* person?
25. If I could rerun my life, what would I do differently? The same?

'Nuff said. This should give you a fairly good profile. The exercise will help you get better acquainted with yourself and it'll clarify your personal needs and aspirations. You'll have a list of likes and dislikes about yourself, your occupation, your organization. Solid material for an action plan. Design your own plan.

Format doesn't matter, but the action, the planning does. You're only a captive of The System if you turn yourself in. You can be free emotionally, if not always economically, provided you're determined to be so and willing to work for the luxury.

Design a road map to guide you through your own organization or into another. Consider forming one of your own, if that route appeals to you. Stay out of limbo. Either know where you want your career to go next, or know that you don't care, that you're willing to go wherever circumstances lead you. But don't get trapped in the middle. Your job performance and treatment of employes will reflect your ambivalence. You could end up being another organizational albatross.

This isn't a guaranteed formula for advancement. There's no such thing. However, periodic self-examinations can aid your promotional progress. What the exercise really delineates is an approach to living—with yourself. Face it: you may never head your organization or any other for that matter. You may be too heavily invested in your current occupation or employer to make a change. Economic realities may impinge on your dreams. But if you understand yourself and your dreams you can develop other outlets—and you can find contentment in your life. Once you do that, your supervisory and other interpersonal relationships take on new meaning and can be a source of genuine personal satisfaction. In that sense, it's never too late.

Your Autobiography

Have you read your autobiography lately? You don't have one, you say? Why not write one?

Probably you never realized before how much writing can be involved in thinking. However, words are concrete on paper, often fuzzy in recollection. Here's an approach:

In as many paragraphs and pages as it takes, note your experiences, your accomplishments, your failures. If you don't have any failures identified and explained by the time you complete the exercise, start over. You've missed the point and left out an

essential ingredient for self-improvement. Everyone could have done something better.

Be sure to include a personality summary. Itemize your strong points and weak points: generosity, congeniality; bad temper, moodiness, etc. Take lots of time on this portion—and be honest, strive for objectivity. Remember, unless you allow them to, no one will read this but you. You can afford to be honest. And if you really want to improve as a person and as a supervisor, you can't afford not to be honest.

When your report is completed you should have a fairly good picture of yourself, provided you've compiled it with a certain degree of detachment, as if it were written by someone else. That's important too. Your goal is a clearer view of where you've been, where you are, what you've done well, what you need to do today and tomorrow as part of your self-improvement program.

Consider the passages regarding personality traits. How many negative points can you detect? Or does this self-evaluation portray you only in positive terms? If so, try again. Try to see yourself as others may. Be candid. Be critical.

Good biography requires research. Supplement your own evaluation by some conversation with others. Attempt to discover what friends and associates think of you as a person. In the case of peers, how do they rate you as a supervisor? As a person? A note of caution here: Be as subtle as you can, otherwise, people may be apt to tell you what they think you want to hear.

Talk with some of your employes. They're rating you as a supervisor all the time. You may as well discover their opinions and put them to use. Again, handle this delicately so you'll end up with useful information.

When you complete these two exercises, compare the results with your self-evaluation. At the least, you'll learn where your image with other people differs from your own view. And you'll surely uncover some revelations regarding your management methods.

Presumably, you receive periodic evaluations from your boss. If not, you should. However, more often than not, these won't provide all the information you require. For instance, since you're a supervisor, your appraisal may cover the performance of your work group, rather than your role and characteristics as its leader. The difference may seem subtle, but there's a real distinction. For one thing, you already know how well your group has done over, say, the last year. What you don't know is your boss's opinion on whether you've grown as a supervisor.

- Are you closer to promotion this year than you were last year?
- Are you considered a backup candidate for your manager's job?
- What does your boss believe are your strong and weak areas as a supervisor?

If your group's performance was excellent during the period covered by your appraisal, your boss may say so and perhaps a lot of other flattering things too. What he may not say is what you really need to know: what went wrong.

None of us is so incisive that we know precisely and completely every area in which we must improve in order to advance in the organization. Appraisal time is the time to find out. Push your boss to give you all the news—good and bad. And get it in writing so you'll have some additional information to deposit in your personal data bank.*

Of course, an effective manager appraises his employes and himself all the time. You should know almost on a daily basis where you stand. If you don't have that kind of relationship, you, your boss, and the organization all are being cheated. Probably by yourselves.

Using your own evaluation, plus the opinions of others, you can begin to build a model for the future you. What's left to complete the design is an *extremely* subjective and personal input. So much so that you may find it an embarrassing or even silly exercise. Try it anyhow. Remember, no one but you will see this.

Your Eulogy

On a separate sheet of paper write your own eulogy. So it sounds silly. So what? What can you lose? And you may gain something.

On your paper, write the words you'd like to hear uttered over your grave. What would you like to be remembered for? Fairness? Courage? Wisdom? Make it a flowery speech—the kind that has secretly thrilled you when similar words were said of someone else. When you finish, go back, pull out and list the personal characteristics contained in the eulogy. Now match them against your self-evaluation and the survey of other people you conducted. You now have three useful inputs for a success model: self-evaluation, outside opinions, an ideal.

---

* Here's another test of guts, for you *and* your boss.

While it's true that circumstances may preclude your becoming *what you want*, you can influence *who you are*. Many people act as if this weren't so, perhaps because they simply don't believe they can affect their own personalities. Consequently, they don't try. But it can be done.

Once you take the time for the analysis of your personal characteristics and behavior, you acquire a better understanding of yourself both as a person and as a supervisor. Then, having set some personality goals for yourself, you can create a model for your own behavior. This model will help you react the way you truly want to in many interpersonal situations. Not all, but enough to make the effort rewarding.

You can employ these exercises independently or combine elements of one approach with those of another. That's Mix. The Match occurs when you compare likes and dislikes, assets and liabilities, goals, accomplishments and setbacks, your past and your present—and your prospects.

Whatever method you choose will require hard work. The exercises may even be a little painful at first, at least until you begin to feel the rewards of contentment and of improved interpersonal relationships.

Or you can choose to do nothing, which is usually the case for most people. However, if that's your election, you may well deny yourself the pleasure of getting to know a fairly nice person: you.

Chapter 14

Parochialism—The Enemy Within

Characteristics of Parochialism

Parochialism operates like a virus. It's an insidious invader that can infect any organization. It attacks the attitudes and affects the actions of many individuals and work groups.

In the work place, parochialism goes beyond "narrowness of interest," the term's common meaning. Instead, we see parochialism expressed as extreme selfishness. It's characterized by disinterest in, and even disregard for, the concerns, efforts, and aspirations of other individuals and work groups. Unfortunately, it's like a head cold, by the time you realize you're getting it, you've got it.

Employes of a parochial group (P.G.) usually are:

- Resistant to ideas and suggestions from people outside their group. This is the infamous "not invented here" (NIH) factor.
- Extremely sensitive. They are defensive in dealing with criticism, no matter how mild or constructive. Overreaction and counterattack are common responses to criticism.
- Openly critical of the shortcomings of other groups and their employes.

- Reluctant to cooperate with others. They attempt to go it alone, even when assigned by management to a multigroup team effort. This is especially true when the P.G. is not the team leader. Should the project or other effort fail, P.G. people rationalize their role by minimizing their impact. Had they been permitted greater influence, they assert, the failure would have been avoided.
- Cautious, even secretive, about sharing information—to the point of dispensing little that is valuable.
- Careful to conceal facts and figures which may reflect unfavorably on the group's performance. Even a forecasted schedule delay or budget overrun (no matter how slight) will be disguised to avert management scrutiny.
- The palace guards of prerogatives, fiercely defending their group's "charter" against any intrusion.
- More concerned with supremacy over co-components than over external competitors.
- Jealous of the successes and smug regarding the failures of other groups.
- Quick to claim credit for the success of a multigroup team effort, even where the P.G. has hindered more than helped.

- Condescending as hell. They attitudinally portray a position that theirs are the only people who know anything. They routinely and vocally lament the "fact" that everyone else's incompetence necessitates that the P.G. "carry" the organization. P.G. people are really put-upon!

Most work groups have a person or two who behaves this way with varying degrees of frequency and tenacity. In truth, we all occasionally display one or more of these characteristics. It's only when a few are combined to form a behavioral pattern that they become troublesome, even dangerous to individual development and organizational health.

Parochialism is a dirty 12-letter word. (That makes it three times worse than a dirty four-letter word.) Worse yet, parochialism is learned behavior.

How It Develops

Our social value system encourages individual accomplishment. Our cultural heroes are those who acquire the most wealth or other forms of recognition. We also stress fidelity toward the small groups we call family and friends. Society offers few tangible rewards for altruism. The altruist's rewards generally must come from within. Conceivably, one reason why so few Albert Schweitzers emerge.

We're all products of our environment and our experiences. Our organizations are actually small societies—miniature mirrors of the larger entity. Therefore, it's not surprising that the social characteristics which influence our development as individuals also affect our development and maintenance of working relationships. We prefer people with whom we share interests. We're loyal to those we know and like best.

Disclaimers to the contrary, we're "honest and open" with only a few people. We tend to distrust strangers, and we seldom rely on a person before getting to know him well. One major exception: Ironically, as supervisors, we frequently entrust job assignments affecting the welfare of both the organization and ourselves to veritable strangers. We call them employes.

People cling to groups, including their work groups, for the same reason they formed tribes: security. Besides, *one* is a very lonely unit. We seek companionship and comfort too. In private life, we achieve these goals through relationships with family and friends. In such relationships, we find trust (security) and common interests and experiences (companionship). We fulfill needs to express and *be* ourselves without fear of rejection. We have the opportunity to share—physically, emotionally, spiritually—with other people in an honest, open, and unembarrassed way (comfort).

Avoiding It

When our relationships with others are in fact honest, open, and equitable in the sharing aspect, we are rewarded. We feel important, needed. They raise our self esteem. We are more important to ourselves (in the healthy and wholesome sense) when we perceive ourselves as valuable to others.

Such feelings support a person's basic drive for recognition. "I exist. I am here. Now. I contribute. I matter." Among the counterpoints to this drive are fear, anxiety, frustration, stress, and feelings of inadequacy. Too often in organizational life it's these feelings which dominate a person as he acts, reacts and interacts with other people.

Where organization managers create or maintain an environment characterized by fear, distrust, or uncertainty; or where they display or countenance excessively authoritarian behavior, then parochialism, with all its negative implications, is sure to run rampant. People will find security, acceptance, recognition, and the rest in small groups and "act out" their hostility with employes outside their group.

Parochial groups merely take on personalities which reflect the fears, animosities, and insecurities of the individual members. Individual insecurity may masquerade as group loyalty, but it's likely that each member will be mentally looking over his shoulder, watching the others with some suspicion.

Eventually, the need for shelter which leads to parochial group behavior—and which results in its superficial appearance of member fidelity—gives way to the individual self-interest that spawned it. The cycle comes full turn.

Groups behave as people because organizations are people.

When supervisors are themselves threatened, insecure, and uncertain of their ability to survive the rigors of management, their behavior—self-seeking, secretive, surly in interpersonal situations—can stimulate the growth of employe self-interest and protectiveness which sprouts into parochialism. Employes quickly perceive their superior's position and usually follow his lead.

Most supervisors, and all good ones, work to instill a sense of group pride and loyalty in their employes. Occasionally, some employes may misread a signal and start cutting a path toward parochialism. However, the supervisor who knows his people and maintains proper peer relationships can alter their course before they've travelled too far.

Too often, though, supervisors are so busy pushing paper or chasing hardware that they know little about their employes as individuals and even less about what group gamesmanship they may be up to. Not until there's a problem, that is. There's always time to fix problems, never enough to know people. For some reason, we seldom act as if *prevention* were part of the problem-solving function.

It may appear that the existence or absence of parochialism in certain of your organizational components doesn't matter one way or another. You might argue that many groups are never called on to perform as team members; that they have little contact with customers, the public, or even other employes. This may be so as regards external contacts. However, everyone's output is someone's input. Therefore every person, every group is a team member.

Every group's output makes contact with other people, affects the successful operation of the organization. If this is not the case, why are these groups in place? Why are their employes on the payroll?

All employes have "mental contact" with others in the organization. Certain employes may work in relative seclusion, even isolation, due to the nature of their jobs. But they still see and hear things about the people and operations of other groups. Many employes are friends; associate frequently outside the work place.

Employes are aware of their organizational environment. They form impressions. They exchange information. They evaluate their own supervisor and those who head other components.

While many employes cannot always see the end result of their labor, they "see" mentally the kind of outfit and kinds of people they work for and with. So unless you want employes to "go into business for themselves," but on your time and payroll, you'll devise ways to integrate their self-interest with your organization's objectives and with the efforts of other groups.

Chapter 15

Creating a Climate for Understanding

Throughout this book, we've focused on individual actions required to make our organizations habitable by human beings. These actions must be initiated by us, as supervisors, since we are at least the nominal leaders of our organizations. Leadership always imposes responsibilities. It is alternatively a source of rewards and a burden. Sometimes, it's an outright drag. But to accept the rewards without assuming the responsibilities is yet another rip-off.

Another recurring theme has to do with understanding and the relationships which foster understanding between people. For our purposes, that's what communication is all about. This point has been stressed, perhaps even hammered. However, communication is like sex in one respect: It's possible to have too much, but you never get enough.

As noted earlier, personal relationships are an integral part of organizations. Open your door for business and relationships are there waiting to happen. However, their nature, quality, and contributive value to the organization depends on the kind of climate established and maintained by the management.

Setting the Climate

What follows are some thoughts on climate-setting. Regard them as a menu or shopping list. Pick and choose those that apply to your organization or circumstances. Choose carefully, though. Don't reject something because "that's not the way we do it here." That's a cop-out. It also reflects an attitude that causes many of corporate America's biggest—and clearly self-imposed—problems.

You'll find nothing magic here. Numerous factors can and will influence your success as you strive to enhance the environment in which you work. However, it's certain that results are contingent on your hard work and on your awareness. The latter should cause you to apply thoughtfully your knowledge regarding individual self-interest, self-esteem, and self-concept. Provided you creatively utilize this knowledge in ways which minimize individual and group parochialism—thus making the "selfs" work for you—you will be at least moderately successful. Cooperation among employes will increase, relationships between you and your associates will improve.

Consider some things you can do today to brighten and warm your organization's communication climate, now and for the future.

Make each employe responsible for his job and his performance.

You may be surprised to learn that many employes don't know what you expect of them. Some may even confide that they're not really sure what their job is. Curiously, this also applies to some high-level managers.

It's an excellent investment of your time to have a conversation on the subject of his job with each employe who reports to you. Set standards. Assure him and yourself that each of you understands what is expected *of the other*. This last phrase is crucial. Employes have expectations too. Know what they are. Expectations influence employe attitudes and performance. They also affect the communication climate you share.

Make it clear to employes that performance will be measured and that, insofar as it's within your control, pay increases, promotions, even retention, will depend on performance.

At the same time point out that when you help an employe with a problem you're also helping yourself, the work group, and the entire organization. Use all available means to remove employe reluctance toward discussing problems or other kinds of "bad news." Don't let a person feel alone with his problem. It's costing you money.

Remove negative threat from the environment. We're all subject to disciplinary action and dismissal. We all know it. These are threats, but the kind we can live with. Responsible people accept them as reasonable in an organized society. The knowledge seldom is damaging, even though it's threatening. Constant reminders, however, smack of intimidation. They create negative pressure, and this nearly always damages people and their relationships.

Each organization has its own rules regarding discipline, some of them quite arbitrary. Each manager has his own views, some of them quite arbitrary. But arbitrariness is yet another enemy of communication. Eliminate it. Explain the organization's law to employes. Describe the ground rules you believe should apply in your work relationship. Discuss them. Get your employes' views—and make sure they understand yours. In this way, and of course through your subsequent behavior, employes will be assured that you're not one of those management maniacs who shoots the messenger who brings the bad news. Not all news can be good. Mistakes will occur. Problems will arise. The sooner these come to your attention, the quicker you can get involved. The greater your lead-time, the more efficiently you can remedy a situation.

Some employes feel more comfortable when they have a document which delineates their responsibilities and the basic points on which they'll be measured, evaluated, appraised—whatever term you like. Call it a job description, job statement, or position guide. It's a kind of contract between supervisors and their employes. It specifies how employes can succeed or fail on the job. And it serves as a handy reference in time of doubt. Other employes may not care about a written position guide so long as they have sufficient contact with their supervisor to gain an understanding of what the job—and the supervisor—are all about.

If your organization doesn't have a policy on this, you may find that offering employes in your group an option opens a new avenue of trust. The major thing, however—whatever the policy or your position—is to have the conversation. And repeat it periodically.

Conduct periodic performance reviews.

Your organization may have a policy which mandates periodic performance documentation and discussion with employes. Fine, but don't rely exclusively on this procedure. Some reasons why you shouldn't:

- If you get busy with other things, you'll probably slip the reviews or ignore them altogether.
- You may be conscientious about doing the appraisals and conducting the conversations which accompany them, but if this is your major contact with employes in an off-the-firing-line setting, not much of lasting value will transpire. They'll be up-tight, you'll be less than relaxed (mostly because you won't know each other), and little communication will occur.
- If you're generally pleased with an employe's work, why wait six months to a year to discuss and fix a thing or two you're perhaps dissatisfied with?
- If you're generally pleased with an employe's work you probably won't put in writing what you would—or should—let him know about his faults during a conversation. No sense blemishing his record, damaging his career.

There should never be a time when an employe doesn't know the areas of his performance which you rate as good (or better), satisfactory, or poor (if applicable). He should always be aware of his strengths and weaknesses—especially the items requiring improvement. Today, your opinion and his are the ones that matter most.

It's important also that you be as complimentary as you are critical. True, no one's all good. Conversely, no one's all bad either. If an employe's performance is consistently poor, why is he still on your payroll?

For criticism to be effective, it must be balanced by compliments. And compliments must be real, not flattering fluff; earned, not gratuitously dispensed.

Balance is the key. If you praise people with near-equal enthusiasm for every accomplishment, ranging from trivial to extraordinary, you and your compliments will eventually forfeit credibility. The inspirational effect will be lost, and your integrity may be questioned.

There's another risk too. Constant praise creates an unreal atmosphere. A sudden invasion by even a mild criticism can have an unduly deflating effect on certain employes. On the other hand, constant criticism, without the intervention of occasional praise, injects people with an intellectual and emotional immunity. Constant criticism violates their self-concept; evokes cynicism. People know they're not "bad" all the time. A supervisor's failure to maintain balance can create a climate in which his messages are automatically rejected, his purposes defeated, and, eventually, his credibility destroyed.

When appraising an employe, be sure to evaluate him as a person in context with his job.

Everyone within the same labor classification, doing a similar job, should have an identical job description. Ostensibly, this provides an objective basis for measuring employe performance. It's not literally objective, but, at least in theory, everyone in the same work category is evaluated against a common standard. If you're using this tool fairly objectively, that's good. But not good enough. Consider this situation:

Two people perform identical duties. One is extremely bright and has super skills. The other is mediocre—"average" IQ and ability. They both do "satisfactory" work when measured against the performance standard in their job guide. . . but. . . the mediocre guy is "busting his chops" while the bright guy is "coasting." What now?

The bright one, it would seem, should be placed on a more demanding job. You should consider that, and discuss it with him at the next appraisal session.

On the immediate problem, though, how do you rate these employes for the record? Is the employe with superior skills "unsatisfactory" because he does "satisfactory" work when, in your opinion, he should be doing "outstanding" work? Is the employe with average skills "outstanding" because he does "satisfactory" work and you find this remarkable?

The answer seems to be "no," in each case. Both employes are "satisfactory" on the rating scale. But don't just check off boxes on some form. Use the narrative technique. In your written appraisal and during the employe discussion session you can give abundant credit and recognition to one employe without demoralizing or otherwise damaging the other. This technique puts the person and his performance in context with his job.

One employe possibly knows he can do better. Whether or not he'll admit it is a matter of his awareness, candor—or perhaps the state of his mental health. Find out. Help out. The other employe may believe he's doing his best. This could well be the case. Let him know that you know—and appreciate his perseverance and his performance.

Most of your employes probably are average—in skill, ability, performance, IQ, attitude, whatever category you name. Most of *us* are average too. But there are among us, and among them, many people who want to do the best job possible. Some know they're not world-beaters. Some don't. All desire economic rewards. All *need* some psychic reward.

A healthy communication climate requires that we recognize and reward people for their attitudes and efforts as well as for their accomplishments.

We live and work at a time when talent, ability, and skill can be easily bought on the open market. Loyalty, perseverance, and initiative are tougher to come by. And respect still must be earned.

Respect is a function of relationship. When you know your employes, their individual aims, aspirations, and achievements; when you understand and acknowledge the dynamics driving their performance, you pay them respect. And that's the best way to earn theirs.

*Make cooperation with other people within and outside the work group part of each employe's job.**

---

* Nothing in this section is intended to discourage *constructive* individual and inter-group competition. Such competition stimulates people, adds zest to the work environment, and can lead to a more profitable enterprise. On the other hand, unregulated competition can resemble guerrilla warfare—with your company becoming the chief casualty.

This prescription, coupled with your personal leadership, offer the most effective inoculation against personal and group parochialism.

Notify employes that cooperation with others is part of their job. Make it clear that this performance point carries equal weight with other measurement criteria. This will establish the letter of the law, if not the spirit. The spirit will follow, provided you don't stop here.

Expect to be tested a few times. On these occasions, when someone doesn't cooperate with another on an assignment (stay out of the petty personal hassles), you'll have to reinforce your point with suitable verbal or other action. In time, and through leadership, it comes.

You'll also want to tell your peers what you're up to. And don't neglect to solicit their support. Other supervisors can provide a vital input regarding cooperation by your employes with theirs.

Urge your peers to inform you of significant incidences of good and poor cooperation. Express an interest in cooperating with them—on projects and in an information exchange. Encourage letters of commendation when appropriate and earned by your people. Send letters to other supervisors when their employes do something extraordinary which benefits your group or a project of mutual group interest.

This is also a subtle way of providing a model for other supervisors who may follow your lead. It may help to overcome some feelings of threat. Your motives are apt to be questioned at first, but that's part of the price of leadership.

Be sure that your employes know what you're up to. Discuss with them areas for improved cooperation with other groups. Get their ideas. The effect of this can be to raise the level of parochialism one organizational notch. There's a way to go yet, but at least at this stage there's *us* and *some* of them.

Initiate an informative exchange.

Enthusiasm and interest stem mostly from curiosity and information. Employes usually have some interest in how other groups function, particularly where the output of one group is the input for another. And many employes are at least moderately interested in the history, overall operations, and product scope of their organization. This may be particularly true for employes of large manufacturing firms. This curiosity, once satisfied, can help people answer the question, "Is what I do for a living in any way worthwhile in the greater scheme of things?"

Variations of this question nibble at more employes—including executives—than just those who admit it. In the cosmic sense, the answer may well be "No." But so far as the success and survival of our organizations is concerned, the answer should be a resounding "Yes!" (Or at least a definite "Maybe.") Many employes lack sufficient information to either decide or appreciate their role.

This is a well-known problem for supervisors of "production" employes. But supervisors of "office" employes face it too. And a lot of "professional" people, including many in management, seem to complain about insufficient information to satisfy their wonderings or optimize their contribution.

Imagine that today is the first day on the job for the employes of your group. They're curious.

- From where does our input come?
- Who manages that component? What's he like?
- What are his employes like?
- What work do they do that we don't get to see?
- What processes do they use to create our input?
- Who gets our output?
- What processes do they use?
- Who runs that component? What's he like?
- What are his people like?
- Who gets *their* output?

Experienced employes usually are familiar with the people and functions of the input and output sides of your group's operations. But don't take too much for granted. Don't assume that employes have all the information they need to either satisfy their curiosity or to do their best work.

Even if your group's input comes from numerous sources, and your output has more than one destination, your employes are likely to be most familiar with those people and processes affecting their own job. If yours is a large group, many of your employes may be virtually ignorant regarding the duties of others in the group—let alone those of outsiders. This is an area worth your attention, particularly where the outsiders can ultimately influence your group's performance.

Go a step further. It's likely that even those employes who are fairly well informed will have only a slight acquaintance with the people and operations *two* component links removed from

yours on the input/output chain. And the further you take it, the greater the slope in the employe knowledge/information curve.

What should you do about this? What can you do?

The answers depend on you, and on the constraints imposed by your group's daily work schedule and your management. However, if you agree that well-informed employes are more interested in their jobs, and thus more productive, you might consider these useful information devices.

Begin by putting yourself in your employes' place. No one likes to feel isolated. And it's dangerous when we become insular. Wouldn't you like to know more about your organization, its objectives, its operations? In fact, don't you share some of those questions we assumed your employes might be asking?

Why not get the answers for yourself and your people? Satisfy your curiosity and theirs. Don't wait for others to come to you. Lead. Take the initiative.

- Identify your input/output associate groups—one *and* two steps removed.
- Arrange periodic meetings with the supervisors of those groups. In certain instances, an individual head-to-head exchange may be appropriate; in others a small group session might be most rewarding.
- Find out their procedures, their problems. Try to discover how they rate your group's performance in cooperative efforts. Where can improvements be made—in their style and yours? Get to know these other supervisors and something about their bosses. Learn their strengths (so you'll know where to get help when you need it), their weaknesses (so you'll know where you and your group must be strong and who may occasionally need your help), and their personality hang-ups (so you'll know how to modulate complaints, criticism and compliments).
- Discuss these meetings, their implications and your insights with your employes. Get their reactions, comments, suggestions, questions. Be prepared for the next meeting.

- Arrange an occasional meeting of your employes and those of other work groups. Encourage people to get to know each other, have their own discussions on cooperative matters. If you can't have all employes off-the-job at the same time, assemble a delegation. This may be "down time" but it's certainly productive time.
- Get other supervisors to brief your group on the responsibilities and operations of their components. These briefings, and the ensuing question-and-answer periods, can enlighten the participants, foster continued cooperation, enhance the communication climate.
- Consider intergroup temporary assignments for certain employes. This is practical where skills are interchangeable and where work schedules and commitments would not be unduly disrupted. Here's a useful technique for building relationships and expanding individual horizons. Don't reject it out of hand.

On the matter of "What's this whole organization all about—and how do I fit in?" there are several ways to go.

- Every organization has someone (or some group) familiar with the history, products, structure, management philosophy, and other aspects of the enterprise. Arrange a presentation for your employes. (You may find this informative yourself.)
- Invite some members of top management to meetings with your group. Better work this one through your boss, though. He may not have read this book and may feel threatened by your mingling with the big guys.
- Discover what, if anything, is bugging your employes. Then either find the answers or send people to the appropriate specialists. If employe questions and/or concerns are of general interest and/or concern, bring the specialists to a group meeting. You're a client to the specialists. Don't be shy. Let 'em earn their money.

Stay tuned-in to the other supervisors who work for your boss.

They're your basic peer group. They can be critical to your success, so it makes sense to establish and maintain the most cooperative peer relationships possible. Let your employes *see* these relationships operate. Once employes observe your cooperation, consideration, and courtesy in peer-group situations, they'll get the message. For many, no other signal will be necessary. They'll follow your example in their peer relationships. When this occurs, the climate is further enhanced.

Utilize, and instill in your employes, the concept of client relationships.

This one's a little tricky. Its feasibility and limits depend on the nature of your work. If your group necessarily operates in a precise, quasi-military manner, some of the following suggestions may be unsuitable. If you're not so constrained, many may be useful. See what applies.

Regard your superior as a client, rather than a boss. Once you make the transition, your attitude toward him and your job changes significantly. He becomes a client, your job becomes a role; your occupation, whatever its label, becomes a profession. The same is true in your relationships with peers, employes, and other associates.

The client concept causes you to expand your perspective and extend your role in the organization. You no longer work *for*, you work *on behalf of*. There's a psychological as well as a semantical difference. It's an approach, not a panacea. You'll still have opinions and suggestions rejected. But you may well find that more are accepted than is now the case. One reason is that the quality of your ideas and other inputs will improve. Another is that you'll be speaking up more, you'll be taking responsibility. Your interest and concern won't be lost on your boss and associates. (That's not all positive, by the way. Some people will feel threatened by you. Expect some hassles with certain associates. You know who they are.)

If this concept seems appealing but unusable because you've got an authoritarian boss or work in a totalitarian organization, you've got five basic choices:

1. Try to change your boss.
2. Form a cadre of like-minded people and operate as best you can.
3. Find a new boss; change jobs.
4. Quit. (It's less traumatic to resign a client than quit a job.)
5. Sit there and suffer.

You do have a choice.

Encourage your employes to think of you and their coworkers as clients. This stimulates cooperation. It's not too way-out either.

In an R & D outfit, for instance, engineering, quality control, and manufacturing must interact. Their cooperative efforts are critical to efficiency and cost-effective performance. Here's a clear case of relationship being built into the organization's structure.

All but the smallest enterprises have someone or some group responsible for accounting/finance, employe relations, facilities maintenance, and other services affecting the overall entity. The client relationship between these people and others in the organization is obvious.

As the client, don't recoil from employe questions which imply criticism. Face them. Evaluate them. Answer them.

Don't wait for suggestions, solicit them. Don't ignore ideas because they're not yours (you're not really that threatened, are you?); capitalize on them where possible and give credit where it's due. Reward initiative, don't trample it.

A cautionary note: If your group or organization is ripe for change, you may have to restrain some overly enthusiastic employes. You can't have everyone charging around doing his own thing. All counsellors, no workers.

Selectively involve your boss in the process.

Determine which (if not all) of the preceding suggestions seem suited to your situation. Assess your prospects for immediate success in implementing them. Formulate a plan for approaching the program. Have a clear idea of your current communication climate. List the problems you share with your boss, peers, employes, and other associates. Consider your own short- and long-range goals. All these factors should influence your plan. *You want to accomplish something.*

When you have the plan, review it with your boss. Get his reactions. Try to get his support. *Do not talk with him about the idea before you have a plan.* It'll sound "flaky"—like a waste of time.

If your boss doesn't like the plan, get his specific objections and suggestions for improvement. If he doesn't like any of it, maybe you've got a poor plan. Or maybe he's got his own hang-ups. Determine which. If he disapproves of the entire idea, discretely do it anyhow. He'll love you later, especially if *his* boss hears what you've been up to—and likes it. (Don't be too surprised at that point if your boss rips off a little credit for the idea. That's show biz.)

In most cases, if you properly present a well-planned program, your boss will cooperate. This opens new avenues of opportunity.

- By notifying the other members of his staff that he supports the approach, he'll instantly reinforce the effort.
- Other staff members will more readily cooperate.
- Hopefully, they'll make similar efforts within their own groups and with their input/output associate groups.
- Your boss will tell his boss and the ripple in the pool may expand.
- Your boss' peers and superiors may be intrigued by the possibility that perhaps the work environment need not be hostile and often unfit for human habitation. They may even get their own thing going.

The greatest immediate benefit will accrue should your boss adopt some program of his own. You and your fellow supervisors may not be much better informed than the average employe. For instance:

- What are your boss' expectations?
- Where do you stand with him?
- How are you measured?
- When did you and your boss have your last "personal" conversation?
- What business is your parent organization in?

And there are spinoffs. An occasional "well done" from your boss to one of your employes, or to the entire group, can have a stimulating effect on morale. It's temporary, but it helps. Periodic visits by him to your work area also help, especially if he takes a moment here and there to chat with employes. Perhaps you'll want to arrange a group meeting with your boss, preferably with you not in attendance. Like hell, you say. You're not really that uptight, are you? Let employes ask The Man some questions. Let him get to know them a little. It's a useful exposure on both sides.

All this takes guts and confidence on your part. The possibilities for success and failure are almost limitless. That's what makes the challenge so attractive.

Establish group performance goals, including one for cooperative efforts with other groups. Periodically measure group accomplishments against these goals.

Every supervisor has quotas or goals to achieve and a budget to live with. Many of these are superimposed on you by higher management. In addition to these obligations, it's useful to commit yourself and your employes to other worthwhile tasks, the accomplishment of which will enhance the group's value to the organization.

A set of group goals encourages teamwork and provides visible targets for every member of the group. Maximize employe involvement in the goal-planning process. They, not you, must do the work.

Goals must be specific, not fuzzy. They must state precisely what is to be achieved. Employe participation in the goal-setting exercise fosters communication, enhances the climate, and improves the odds that goals will be met.

Employes—all of us—know we can't reasonably expect to be involved in every decision. Most of us, however, want some say on our own destiny. The goal-setting exercise affords an opportunity for you to demonstrate your awareness of this human characteristic.

Goals are worthless if performance against them can't be measured. That's another reason why they must be specific. The measurement period must also be specific: a quarter, six months, a year. Individual goals contained in the group plan should be assigned completion dates—milestones. A milestone completed is an achievement. A milestone missed is a warning light which can alert you to goal-related problems while there's still time to fix them.

Periodically, prepare a list of accomplishments. This lets you and your employes see how you're doing on the goals. Here again you'll need employe inputs, and be sure to share the resulting report with them. If the report looks favorable, you'll want to share it with your boss too. If not, you'll want to file it and do better next time; but review this one with him anyhow.

Insert a "cooperation" category in your goals. Otherwise this item may get insufficient attention. People focus on the things they're held accountable for.

Sooner or later some individual's failure to cooperate with others will result in the group's failure to achieve a goal. Here's a check point on the effectiveness of climate setting efforts. Look for peer pressure to bear down on the offender and modify his behavior, if not his attitude. Peer pressure is operating all the time on all of us. It can work *for* us as well.

Individually, these are useful tools for putting human parochial tendencies to work in a constructive fashion. Collectively, they form a programmatic approach toward creating a climate which is conducive to communication in the work place.

Some people may protest: "We don't have all day to stand around communicating." But what else do managers of people have to do? We spend our entire day attempting to communicate in one form or another.

Maybe if we played our communicator role properly we wouldn't require so much time to fix problems which never had to happen in the first place.

Maybe we'd even have a little time to stand around. And maybe the work day wouldn't seem so long.

Epilogue:
Reflections On The Rat Race

Supervisors share a common harassment: pressure. In dealing with daily work, we're usually so occupied by urgent priorities that we ignore essential requirements. Like communication.

Technology increasingly relieves us and our employes of burdensome, time-consuming labor, yet routinely we're hard-pressed to make time for planning, training, or reporting. Consequently, senior managers frequently characterize our efforts in these areas as shoddy, perfunctory, and unintelligible.

We seldom allocate sufficient time to personalize relationships with employes. Nor do we budget much time for self-improvement activities, being still too busy and often too beat at the close of a work day to muster either energy or enthusiasm for such efforts. We must be doing something wrong.

What makes all this work? Where does all the energy go? A lot of it goes down a rathole.

It's possible to run all day and not get anywhere. You can work like hell and not accomplish much of substance. Alternatively, you can manage your component in such a way that more employes seize initiative and enhance their contribution. You'll still have work to do, but it'll be of a more rewarding variety.

Your personality, and to some extent that of your boss, governs the innovative steps you take as a supervisor. If you're uncomfortable in your role, unsure of yourself, unhappy in your career, you'll likely stand still, cast yourself in the concrete of conformity.

If, on the other hand, you crave the responsibilities, risks, and rewards of management and are determined to lead, you can build positive, more productive working relationships. These, of course, depend on communication. Once you accept the notion that communication thrives in a climate of respect—self-respect and mutual respect—you'll make climate-setting a priority, a way of life. And you'll do so even should others around you operate in ways which occasionally create adverse conditions.

Start by assessing your own immediate sphere of influence. What components and people must you interact with? Make a list of employes, superiors, peers with whom you must work closely, harmoniously, if each or any of you is to be effective. Avoid thinking small. Your sphere encompasses more than just your department, division, shop, unit, office, or whatever label identifies the entity you supervise. Cut through your own parochialism. It can cause you to guard your own turf too jealously; to draw in rather than stretch out.

This is a vital first step. Don't ignore it. After you've taken it, try to get others to do the same. Your boss is an excellent candidate. So are your employes and peers.

You'll immediately discover at least two things, both of which may surprise you:

- The number of people on your list who directly affect your ability to do your job efficiently is greater than you think.
- If you succeed in getting other people to make a similar list, communication within each sphere of influence will improve immediately.

Once people appreciate how dependent they are on one another, the old self-interest/survival instinct takes over. In this case, that's the vital second step.

Having done only this much, you'll have extended your sphere and increased your contribution to your organization.

These steps only get you started. However, unless you see yourself as just another person who jockeys hardware through the shop or who pushes paper, you'll take some more.

As a supervisor of people, you know that, unlike paper, people push back. You know also that as quickly as you fix one problem another takes its place. Such is the nature of individuals and institutions.

It's axiomatic: a supervisor's job is to solve problems; that is, to keep things running as smoothly as possible. All problems are people problems, and all people problems involve communication. Why not solve a few problems before they happen?

Developing skills and programs to personalize communication in the work place is at first a chore and a challenge. Once acquired, however, the technique leads to numerous rewards. Not the least of these can be a smoother-running organization and even personal advancement. And then there's the matter of job satisfaction.

Job satisfaction is the hallmark of a healthy organization. It doesn't mean that people run out of ambition or that they like each and every task and all the people they work with all the time. To paraphrase Peanuts: Nobody likes everything all the time. People deriving job satisfaction see some value in what they're doing during the work day. For them, it's not drudgery to get up in the morning. And they're not the ones you find queuing up at the time clock or at the office door waiting for the quit whistle to blow. Employes with job satisfaction are getting considerably more than money out of the job. The supervisor who communicates *with* his people, who blends their skills and personalities into a functional team, is building job satisfaction into employe roles. He's enriching his own role in the process.

Behavioral balance is the key to creating a healthy communication climate. Each supervisor must select himself—and to some extent with his employes—a management style which seems most productive and rewarding for the organization and the employes.

Some points to keep in mind while making your choice:

- Most people don't go to work in order to play. They go to earn a living. They also seek psychic rewards. Most people go to work with the hope of doing something meaningful for themselves and their employer. Therefore, should you treat your employes as if they're under custodial care—infantile participants in some corporate baby-sitting service—you should expect much infantile behavior, mediocre performance, less than full productivity.
- Most people, and all mentally healthy people, have some regard for themselves. They perceive themselves as basically "good" people. They believe they're worth something to themselves and to others. They see themselves as deserving of a certain amount of respect and as capable of making some contribution for which reward should be forthcoming. (Recognize that there will always be some disparity, ranging from slight to great, between what an employe believes is his contribution, his potential, and his just due and what you believe is appropriate.)
- Few people are on a Jekyll-and-Hyde trip. Most do not become somebody else when they arrive at work. Certainly we adjust our behavior to accommodate work rules, peer pressures, and job requirements, but these adjustments are superficial, reflecting what we *do*, not who we *are*.
- Communication flourishes in an environment which combines creative challenge; clear and understandable goals; intelligently conceived assignments; intelligible instructions; the opportunity for success, failure, and another chance; some stability, and some discipline fairly administered.
- Structure and order are essential for the maintenance of institutions. They're also protectors of a human's psyche. Peo-

ple require certain amounts of routine work as a respite from the rigors of exceptional challenge. Few people can work constantly at the limit of their creative capacity. But an overabundance of structure and order creates routine, dull jobs. The supervisor's challenge is to locate the balance point for each employe and for the work group as a unit.

- Communication suffocates in a climate characterized by excessive discipline and authoritarian rigidity. It's also smothered by chaos, which is equally suppressive of employe needs. When a supervisor is unresponsive to employes' needs for recognition, communication becomes impossible. A supervisor who rewards everyone for everything is as bad as the supervisor who rewards no one for anything. Work which is always routine or performed in a climate of ritualistic adherence to trivial work rules is unrewarding, and usually will be accomplished with mediocre competence.
- The best discipline is self-discipline. Without it there would be no literature, no music, no works of art, and very little in the way of technical invention—the kind that provides the purpose for your organization and jobs for you and your employes. Invention is dreamed, then developed through hard work, usually by an individual. It's rarely coerced from a person.
- Excessive discipline degrades a person. This degradation contradicts his self-concept, attacks his self-esteem. Losses here are frequently replaced by hostility. A person who loses respect for himself loses respect for others. It's an easy course, once begun; altering it can be among your most difficult tasks. Why let it begin?

The hostility that employes develop as a result of their supervisor's unnecessarily severe management practices affects their regard for the entire organization. To your employes, you *are* the organization. Animosities aroused by poor relationships within your group may be aimed at you, but it's a shotgun war; the pellets will surely affect productivity.

The foregoing are challenges and opportunities. They challenge you to accept your employes as adult participants in a joint pursuit of organizational, work-group, and individual objectives. By providing employes the opportunity to succeed you will succeed yourself. As a minimum reward you'll have a more interesting job. You'll also achieve job satisfaction by helping employes grow and by contributing to a healthier organizational environment. It may be some time before we see "return on human investment" in the annual report, but when we do, you'll know you helped to put it there. So much for idealism.

That's the long range. For now, your attention to personalized communication practices can increase productivity and decrease the amount of time you spend on petty hassles. Even more rewarding, you'll find that when you take a chance and treat employes as adults, most of these employes will surprise you and *act* as adults. Since most surprises you get are probably bad news, you'll find this one refreshing. Your job will become more difficult in the sense that you'll have more suggestions to discuss and evaluate, more employe initiative to sometimes stimulate, sometimes bridle. And certainly you'll need to communicate more with each individual. But you'll be better informed, more respected, and infinitely more satisfied at the end of the work day. You'll also be out of the rat race. That's yet another reward since, as a friend once remarked: The real problem with being in the rat race is that, win or lose, you're still a rodent.

For supervisors—the strength of an organization and its real men and women in the middle—personalized communication should be a primary professional and personal goal. This goal can be achieved through the same diligence and hard work that leads to the attainment of other skills. The task, therefore, certainly is surmountable. It's a kind of sweat equity: What you put in, you get back. But the burden rests with you.

Unfortunately, there are no foolproof formulas for success as a communicator, no simple solutions for your problems, no magic sand to sprinkle on them and make them disappear. To the extent that you're willing to sensitize yourself to the communication (human) problems within your group and organization and to do something about them, this book hopefully will help. That's all anyone should expect.

No author can make someone else a better communicator. If he does his job well, the author can point a path, perhaps even inspire some action by igniting the reader's imagination. However, it's for you to decide your own destiny.

Only you can decide if you're willing to take the time, exert the effort, bear the frustrations, and suffer the failures prerequisite to the personal satisfaction and other rewards reserved for successful communicators.

It's only right that it should be that way.